Cambridge Elements

Elements in the Renaissance
edited by
John Henderson
Birkbeck, University of London, and Wolfson College, University of Cambridge
Jonathan K. Nelson
Syracuse University Florence

THE MANY LIVES OF TÄSFA ṢEYON

An Ethiopian Intellectual in Early Modern Rome

Matteo Salvadore
American University of Sharjah

James De Lorenzi
City University of New York

Deresse Ayenachew Woldetsadik
Aix-Marseille University

Shaftesbury Road, Cambridge CB2 8EA, United Kingdom

One Liberty Plaza, 20th Floor, New York, NY 10006, USA

477 Williamstown Road, Port Melbourne, VIC 3207, Australia

314–321, 3rd Floor, Plot 3, Splendor Forum, Jasola District Centre,
New Delhi – 110025, India

103 Penang Road, #05–06/07, Visioncrest Commercial, Singapore 238467

Cambridge University Press is part of Cambridge University Press & Assessment,
a department of the University of Cambridge.

We share the University's mission to contribute to society through the pursuit of
education, learning and research at the highest international levels of excellence.

www.cambridge.org
Information on this title: www.cambridge.org/9781009595674

DOI: 10.1017/9781009595681

© Matteo Salvadore, James De Lorenzi and Deresse Ayenachew Woldetsadik 2024

This publication is in copyright. Subject to statutory exception and to the provisions of relevant collective licensing agreements, no reproduction of any part may take place without the written permission of Cambridge University Press & Assessment.

When citing this work, please include a reference to the DOI 10.1017/9781009595681

First published 2024

A catalogue record for this publication is available from the British Library

ISBN 978-1-009-59567-4 Hardback
ISBN 978-1-009-59570-4 Paperback
ISSN 2631-9101 (online)
ISSN 2631-9098 (print)

Additional resources for this publication at www.cambridge.org/Salvadore

Cambridge University Press & Assessment has no responsibility for the persistence or accuracy of URLs for external or third-party internet websites referred to in this publication and does not guarantee that any content on such websites is, or will remain, accurate or appropriate.

The Many Lives of Täsfa Ṣeyon

An Ethiopian Intellectual in Early Modern Rome

Elements in the Renaissance

DOI: 10.1017/9781009595681
First published online: December 2024

Matteo Salvadore
American University of Sharjah

James De Lorenzi
City University of New York

Deresse Ayenachew Woldetsadik
Aix-Marseille University

Author for correspondence: Matteo Salvadore, salvadorematteo@gmail.com

Abstract: This Element examines the life and legacy of the sixteenth-century Ethiopian intellectual Täsfa Ṣeyon. It reconstructs his formative years in the Horn of Africa and his diasporic life in the Holy Land and Italian peninsula, where he emerged as a prominent intermediary figure at Santo Stefano degli Abissini, an Ethiopian monastery within the Vatican. He became a librarian, copyist, teacher, translator, author, and community leader, as well as a prominent advisor to European humanist scholars and Tridentine Church authorities concerned with the emerging field of philologia sacra as it pertained to Ethiopian Orthodox (*täwaḥedo*) Christianity. The Element reconstructs his wide-ranging contacts with the Roman Curia and emerging orientalist academy, and then scrutinizes his *editio princeps* of the Ge'ez Gospels. A final section traces his modern influence, erasure, and rediscovery by later generations of European, Ethiopian, and Eritrean intellectuals.

Keywords: Ethiopian diaspora, Ethiopian intellectuals, orientalism, Eastern Churches, Jesuit missions

© Matteo Salvadore, James De Lorenzi and Deresse Ayenachew Woldetsadik 2024

ISBNs: 9781009595674 (HB), 9781009595704 (PB), 9781009595681 (OC)
ISSNs: 2631-9101 (online), 2631-9098 (print)

Contents

1 Introduction   1

2 The Pious Stranger   6

3 The *mämher* of Rome   23

4 The Influencer   46

5 Rediscoveries   66

  Glossary   87

  Bibliography   89

An online appendix for this publication can be accessed at www.cambridge.org/Salvadore

1 Introduction

After the death of Pope Paul III in November 1549, the College of Cardinals of the Catholic Church entered an unprecedented two-month conclave. It only ended in February, when the scandalous Giovanni Maria Ciocchi del Monte (1487–1555) became Pope Julius III.[1] As the faithful waited, the secluded cardinals produced sixty inconclusive ballots. Their protracted deliberations reflected the deep divisions within the College, encompassing disagreements over the Vatican response to the Protestant Reformation as well as rivalries between supporters of the Holy Roman Empire and the Kingdom of France.[2] After five fruitless weeks, on January 7 a participant reported that an irate African emerged at a balcony within the Sistine Chapel and exclaimed: "Very Reverend Lords, the conclavists have shut the doors, and thus now you must either starve or arrive at a decision about choosing a pope[!]"[3] For some of those present, the outburst was surely a shock. But for the witness and much of the Roman Curia, the interlocutor was a familiar figure: it was Täsfa Ṣeyon (1510–52),[4] the Ethiopian monk widely known to Europeans as Pietro Abissino or Petrus Ethyops.[5] No interloper, he was a conclave sacrist, client of the deceased pope, and powerful advisor to the Tridentine Catholic elite. Indeed, his proximity to Paul III was such that he attended the latter's funeral wearing the ceremonial black cloth reserved for personal friends of the pontiff.[6] The interjection thus came from a grieving member of the *familia papae* at the innermost circles of Vatican power.

Täsfa Ṣeyon hailed from the Horn of Africa. Fleeing the regional conflict between the Christian kingdom of Ethiopia and nearby Sultanate of Adal, he reached the Italian peninsula in the mid-1530s, where he was greeted by Rome's small community of diasporic Ethiopian and Eastern Christians. He became ensconced at Santo Stefano degli Abissini, an Ethiopian monastery within the

---

[1] Dates in parentheses correspond to birth and death, except for heads of churches and states, in which case they delimit time in office. Ethiopian emperors are identified by baptismal name. The authors thank Abebe Ambatchew, Gianfranco Armando, Cristelle Baskins, Andrea Bernardini, *abba* Daniel Assefa, abba Hailemikael Beraki Hasho, Ruth Iyob, Sam Kennerley, Mark Nolan, Alina Payne, Bertie Pearson, Delio Vania Proverbio, Andreina Rita, Cesare Santus, Mark Shockley, Sandro Triulzi, Hamza Zafer, and Ermias Zemichael. This research was funded by two American Philosophical Society Franklin Research Grants, an American University of Sharjah Faculty Research Grant (FRG19-M-S17), a I Tatti Berenson Fellowship, a I Tatti/Getty Foundation Fellowship, and a CUNY John Jay Office for the Advancement of Research grant.
[2] Pastor, *Popes*, Vol. 13, 1–44.
[3] Pietro Paolo Gualtieri's conclave diary, in Merkle, *Concilium Tridentinum*, Vol. 2, 87.
[4] Ge'ez, Amharic, and Tigrinya transliteration uses a simplified version of the *Journal of Ethiopian Studies* system. Arabic transliteration uses the Library of Congress system. Armenian transliteration uses the *Revue des études arméniennes* system.
[5] Angelo Massarelli's conclave diary, in Merkle, *Concilium Tridentinum*, Vol. 2, 126–28.
[6] Merkle, *Concilium Tridentinum*, Vol. 2, 15.

walls of the Vatican, and quickly distinguished himself through his multilingual erudition, entrepreneurial spirit, and political acumen, ultimately becoming a familiar of Alessandro Farnese (1468–1549), who as Pope Paul III (1534–49) sponsored a coordinated Vatican effort to study Ethiopia and its distinctive Orthodox Christian tradition. Along the way, Täsfa Ṣeyon met leading Renaissance humanists, published the *editio princeps* of the Ge'ez New Testament, and instructed luminaries like Ignatius of Loyola (1491–56) and Guillaume Postel (1510–81). In the centuries after his death, the corpus of texts he produced became the foundation of Ethiopia-focused research in Europe, a key branch of the developing field of orientalist knowledge. As his intercession at the Sistine Chapel suggests, Täsfa Ṣeyon was the most influential African in the sixteenth-century Catholic Church.

This Element seeks to understand the fullness of this history, exploring the life and afterlives of Täsfa Ṣeyon as global microhistory. No other diasporic African in early modern Europe approached his position of power and influence. Over the course of two decades, he became the leader of Rome's Ethiopian community, its smallest and most visible extra-European *natio*, and he successfully allied himself with the city's religious and cultural elite, working as a librarian, copyist, teacher, translator, author, and community leader, and advising scholars and church authorities concerned with key areas of orientalist inquiry, from philology to missiology and historiography. Across these different domains, he mobilized his identity as an erudite stranger[7] to further his goal of renewing Ethiopia and Ethiopian Christianity. In 1924, nearly four centuries after his death, the Ethiopian writer Ḥeruy Wäldä Śellasé (1878–1938) described Täsfa Ṣeyon as a diasporic testament to the enduring power of faith, and almost a century later, in 2020, Pope Francis (2013–) celebrated him as a paragon of intercultural ecumenism and the universal church. A sixteenth-century emigrant thus became a synecdoche for Ethiopia's place in the world. In all these respects, his biography illustrates the contemporary reverberations of early modern connected history.[8]

Beyond Exceptionalism

Despite his prominence in Renaissance Rome, Täsfa Ṣeyon has remained on the edges of academic research. With respect to Ethiopian and African historiography, this marginality reflects the evolving intellectual politics of disciplinary orientalism, the genealogy of which we sketch in Section 5. More broadly, the field of African diaspora studies long focused on the larger Atlantic and Indian Ocean cases, with comparatively less attention paid to their Mediterranean and European counterparts.

---

[7] Simmel, "Stranger."   [8] Subrahmanyam, "Connected Histories."

For this reason, the relatively small Ethiopian diaspora of early modern Europe has rarely been studied as a distinctive African diaspora population or adequately situated within broader theorizations of African diaspora history, despite the abundant source material in Ethiopian and European languages.[9] Moreover, much of the extant research is dated and underdeveloped.[10] Earlier generations of church scholars and orientalists edited and translated documents related to the Santo Stefano community, but they did not treat its members as historical agents and frequently adopted a paternalistic heuristic of perennial Italo-African fraternity.[11] Later specialists tended to replicate this ahistorical paradigm,[12] with some notable exceptions.[13] We address these lacunae through an interdisciplinary and multilingual approach, building upon the emerging specialist literature dedicated to the Ethiopian presence in early modern Europe[14] and the early history of Ethiopian–European relations.[15] At the same time, we re-situate Täsfa Ṣeyon within African history, as an attestation of the sixteenth-century global conjuncture of empire in the Horn and the intellectual dynamism of the Ethiopian *liqawent*, or church scholars, in the face of war and collective hardship. Täsfa Ṣeyon played an important role in these momentous developments, and through his attempts to intervene from abroad in events at home, he articulated a new vernacular of Ethiopian diasporic identity.

We suspect these analytic lacunae reflect the enduring perception that Ethiopia is in Africa but not part of it – an exquisitely orientalist understanding of exceptionality that has long underpinned the academic study of Ethiopia, "medieval" or otherwise.[16] This Eurocentric position compounds the challenge of understanding the particularity and interconnectedness of African diasporic

---

[9] For example, Otele, *African Europeans*; Manning, *African Diaspora*; and Earle and Lowe, eds., *Black Africans*.

[10] An important exception is Kelly, *Translating Faith*, which appeared while this Element was under review.

[11] Beccari, *Rerum Aethiopicarum*; Chaîne, "Santo Stefano"; Ignatius Ortiz de Urbina, "Santa Sede"; Euringer, "Tasfa Sejon"; Grébaut, "San-Stefano-dei-Mori"; Guidi, "Nuovo Testamento"; Mauro da Leonessa, *Santo Stefano*.

[12] Lefevre, "Riflessi etiopici ... Parte Prima"; Lefevre, "Riflessi etiopici ... Parte Seconda"; Lefevre, "Riflessi etiopici ... Parte Terza"; Lefevre, "Tasfa Seyon."

[13] Northrup, *Africa's Discovery*.

[14] Kelly, "Ethiopian Diasporas"; Kelly and Nosnitsin, "Two Yoḥannəses"; Kennerley, *Rome and the Maronites*; Salvadore, "Ethiopian Age"; Salvadore, "African Cosmopolitanism"; Salvadore and De Lorenzi, "Täsfa Ṣeyon"; Adankpo-Labadie, "Wandering Lives"; *Encyclopaedia Aethiopica* [hereafter *EA*], Vol. 5, 525–28.

[15] Salvadore, *Prester John*; Krebs, *Ethiopian Kingship*.

[16] Fikru Negash Gebrekidan, "Black Studies"; Teshale Tibebu, "'Anomaly' and 'Paradox'." Illustrating this problem is the historicist periodization of "medieval Ethiopia," which privileges a European referent over Ethiopian, African, or global categories of analysis, and which perpetuates the notion of African relative backwardness. For a critical assessment, see Bausi and Gnisci, "'Medieval' Ethiopia"; and more broadly, Chakrabarty, *Provincializing Europe*.

histories,[17] as is exemplified by the complexity of Täsfa Ṣeyon as a historical subject. Some aspects of his biography seem to personify broader African diaspora experiences. He dedicated his life abroad to preserving his inherited faith and traditions of learning, even as he adapted these to the new intellectual and institutional environment of Catholic Rome. Despite his diasporic "uprootedness," as he termed it in Ge'ez,[18] he was committed to using his distinctive location to defend his ancestral "Mother Ethiopia," as he emotively put it. In other settings, this orientation might be considered a form of creolization. Yet his biography also suggests substantial points of divergence. The documentary record suggests that his life in Europe was rarely touched by the precarity of bondage and enslavement or racialized discrimination based on skin color, even as these defined the experiences of most of his African diasporic contemporaries, Ethiopian or otherwise.[19] He is visually depicted in paintings counseling the most powerful figures in the Catholic Church. Even among diasporic African elites, this level of visibility and evaded disempowerment was unusual.[20] His biography thus differs substantially from that of his better known contemporary Leo Africanus (ca. 1494–ca. 1554), a captive Moroccan diplomat, forced convert, and prolific scholar who introduced Europeans to African history and the Islamic sciences,[21] to say nothing of the iconic eighteenth-century figure of Olaudah Equiano (ca. 1745–97), an Atlantic African author and abolitionist who explicitly imagined his life as an exemplar of broader experiences of diasporic enslavement and survival.[22] These disjunctures risk buttressing the epistemic framework of Ethiopian exceptionalism, obscuring the possibility of understanding Täsfa Ṣeyon within the fullness of Ethiopian as well as African diaspora history, beyond lachrymose and romantic narratives.[23]

As an example of what has been occluded, we document Täsfa Ṣeyon's foundational contribution to the development of Africa-focused orientalism. This contribution was intertwined with the historical and affective conditions of his uprootedness, as is suggested by his innovative language of displacement, which elaborated a scriptural model of Israelite exile and return in dialogue with the collective self-understanding of the Santo Stefano community.[24] In tandem with his *liqawent* training, sharp political acumen, and advanced Latin skills, this diasporic orientation allowed him to shape the institutionalized Vatican effort to produce knowledge about Ethiopian Orthodox Christianity. His stature

---

[17] Gomez, *Reversing Sail*; Manning, *African Diaspora*.
[18] "ኢትዮጵያዊ ፈላሲ [ፈላሲ]." In Ge'ez and Tigrinya, *fälasi* has the secondary meaning of hermit.
[19] Salvadore, "Red Sea"; Salvadore, "António."   [20] Ali, *Malik Ambar*; Wright, *Juan Latino*.
[21] Zemon Davis, *Trickster Travels*; Pouillon et al., *Léon l'Africain*.
[22] Equiano, *Interesting Narrative*, 2.   [23] Iyob, "African Diasporas."
[24] Another member of the community described Moses as "the *liq* of the pilgrims": BAV, Vat. Et. 66, 64v.

as a curial advisor and research collaborator was such that the Ethiopians in Rome awarded him the honorific *mämher*, or teacher, suggesting his critical role in the development of the nascent field of orientalist *philologia sacra*, which sought to deepen European Christian understanding through the comparative study of Eastern Christian languages and texts. This enterprise proved the foundation of the modern academic field of Semitic studies. Yet like Leo Africanus and other sixteenth-century African and Asian intermediaries who educated the first orientalists and translated extra-European texts, Täsfa Ṣeyon's contributions were diminished by later Western specialists who dismissed the authority of these diasporic intellectuals because of their perceived cultural hybridity and proximity to the Catholic missionary enterprise.[25] This erasure fundamentally misconstrues the generative dialectic of orientalism.[26] The early modern meeting of European, African, and Asian minds produced something previously unknown to all: a Western-dominated field of learning predicated on authorial competition, the command of language, and the purported systematic and integrated analysis of extra-European societies through the study of their literature.

Our discussion is based on a variety of archival and published sources, in a range of Ethiopian and European languages. These include Täsfa Ṣeyon's published and unpublished texts; the manuscripts of the Santo Stefano community, in particular a Ge'ez codex that served as its collective history; the archival records of the Vatican support for Täsfa Ṣeyon; and the published and unpublished correspondence and scholarship of curial personalities and researchers that document Täsfa Ṣeyon's activities and influence. The Online Appendix presents original translations of some of these Ge'ez materials. With respect to the modern legacies of this history, our analysis brings together orientalist scholarship, Amharic historiography, the colonial archive, and postcolonial commentaries on Ethiopia's relationship to the West in a range of languages.

Four sections follow. Section 2 examines Täsfa Ṣeyon's life in Ethiopia, emigration to the Holy Land, and subsequent arrival in Rome, where he joined the community of Ethiopian pilgrims at Santo Stefano. Section 3 reconstructs his ensuing intellectual career, from his collaborations with sixteenth-century orientalists and historians to his groundbreaking Ge'ez and Latin publications. Section 4 considers his role as an agent and familiar of Paul III, specifically through his contributions to the construction of the Basilica of Santa Maria degli Angeli e dei Martiri and the planning of the newly established Society of Jesus mission to Ethiopia. Section 5 outlines his posthumous

---

[25] Girard, "Eastern Scholar," 263. [26] Keller and Irigoyen-García, "Introduction."

integration into the orientalist academy, rediscovery by early twentieth-century Ethiopians, and instrumentalization by colonial writers and displaced colonial subjects, concluding with his recuperation as a postcolonial model of intellectual cosmopolitanism and ecumenical fraternity. We hope *The Many Lives of Täsfa Ṣeyon* does justice to this incredibly multifaceted African intellectual.

2 The Pious Stranger

For the people of the Horn of Africa, the sixteenth century was a conjuncture of regional and global conflict. The Ethiopian highlands were then dominated by the Solomonid monarchy, whose dynastic founders claimed lineal descent from the Biblical Solomon and Sheba.[27] Between the thirteenth and fifteenth centuries, this Christian kingdom expanded from its Amhara base to conquer most of the highland plateau, subjugating its Muslim borderlands and establishing garrisons, churches, and monasteries across the new frontier. This process culminated with the reign of Emperor Zär'a Ya'eqob (1434–68), an autocratic reformer who centralized the state, strengthened the church, and elaborated a vision of sacralized royal power rooted in divine election and the symbolic legacy of Aksum.[28] His successors, however, became embroiled in a deepening conflict with the nearby Sultanate of Adal, centered at Harär on the eastern edge of the highland plateau (Figure 1). In the early sixteenth century, its leader 'Aḥmad 'Ibrāhīm al-Ghāzī (1527–43), a charismatic military commander known to Ethiopians as "Grañ," or "the Left Handed," united the Muslims of eastern Ethiopia and present-day Somalia in a campaign to liberate their lost territories, and in 1529, the Adalites defeated the army of Emperor Lebnä Dengel (1508–40). The invaders then swept through the Christian kingdom, decimating its churches and monasteries.

This conflagration quickly involved the larger Ottoman–Portuguese struggle to control the Indian Ocean.[29] In 1535, the beleaguered Ethiopian sovereign requested aid from his Portuguese coreligionists, who were then patrolling the Red Sea in an effort to disrupt its maritime commerce, and six years later, his successor Gälawdéwos (1540–59) welcomed a garrison led by Cristóvão da Gama (1515–42), the son of the Portuguese explorer.[30] The emperor's chronicler found them "thirsty for combat like wolves and hungry for killing like lions."[31] Meanwhile, 'Aḥmad Grañ pledged himself to the Ottoman cause,

---

[27] Taddesse Tamrat, *Church and State*; Derat, *Domaine*.
[28] Crummey, "Solomonic Monarchy"; Deresse Ayenachew, "Territorial Expansion."
[29] Casale, *Ottoman Age*; Subrahmanyam, *Portuguese Empire*.
[30] Martínez d'Alòs-Moner, "Conquistadores." [31] Solomon Gebreyes, *Gälawdewos*, 190.

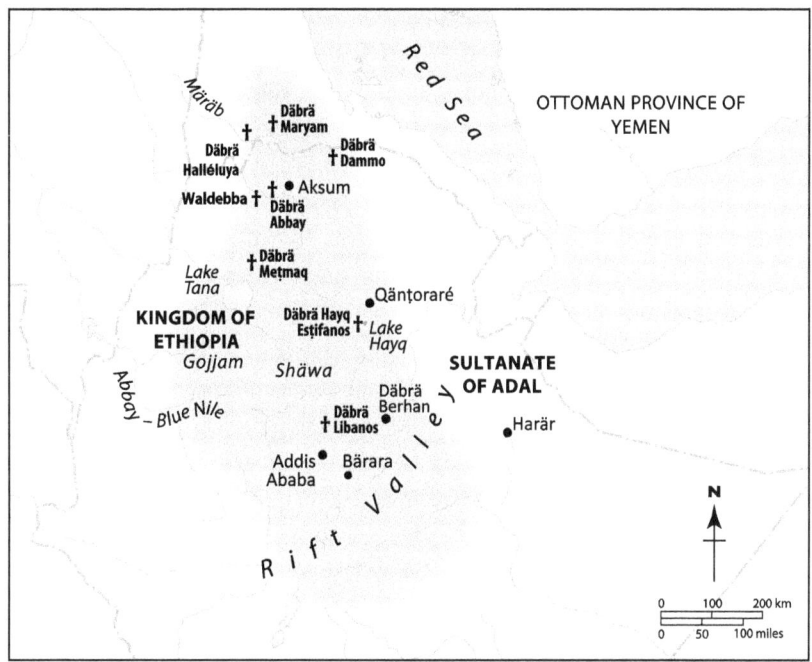

Figure 1 Sixteenth-century Ethiopia (David McCutcheon)

and Istanbul dispatched reinforcements to Adal. These interventions escalated the regional conflict to a proxy war, which ravaged the land for the next two decades. By 1560, it had consumed Gälawdéwos, da Gama, and 'Aḥmad Grañ alike, additionally claiming Özdemir Pasha, the invading Ottoman governor of Yemen. All the while, the kingdom and sultanate faced further attacks by migrating Oromo pastoralists across southern Ethiopia.[32] These were "turbulent times," in the judgment of one Ethiopian witness.[33]

From Däbrä Libanos to Jerusalem

Täsfa Ṣeyon emerged from this era of chaos. Born around 1510, he was initiated as a young man into the rich intellectual culture of Ethiopian Orthodox Christianity. In his later writings, he described himself as an alumnus of Däbrä Libanos monastery, the leading center of church learning in Shäwa and the preeminent religious institution of the land.[34] Founded in the fourteenth century by Saint Täklä Haymanot, Däbrä Libanos played a major role in the religious and political life of the Solomonid kingdom, and its abbot, the *eçhägé*, was the highest-ranking domestic ecclesiastic in the Ethiopian

---

[32] Hassen, *Oromo of Ethiopia*.   [33] Hassen, "Abba Bahrey,'" 277–78.
[34] [Täsfa Ṣeyon], *Testamentum Novum* [hereafter *TN*], 113r, 226v.

church, subordinate only to the Egyptian metropolitan appointed by the Coptic See of Saint Mark in Alexandria.[35] When Täsfa Ṣeyon entered the monastery, it was led by *eçhägé* Enbaqom (ca. 1470–ca. 1560), an erudite Yemeni-Ethiopian convert who later advised Gälawdéwos. With the patronage of Lebnä Dengel, the abbot and brethren presided over a period of Ge'ez literary efflorescence. They standardized the hagiography of their founder Täklä Haymanot, prepared original exegetic works like the anti-Islamic treatise *Anqäṣä amin*, or *Gate of Faith*, and translated works of Arabic Christian literature, such as the commentary of John Chrysostom, the computational treatise of 'Abū Shākir, the pseudo-Buddhist epic Baralaam and Josaphat, and the universal history of Jirjis al-Makīn. In the centuries to come, these became canonical works of Ge'ez literature. As a young initiate, Täsfa Ṣeyon certainly witnessed and perhaps contributed to this project of intercultural textual transmission. In his later years, he pursued this same intellectual project, while invoking *eçhägé* Enbaqom in his writings and adopting the monastic titles *mämher* and *qomos*, or high priest. All this suggests a distinctive erudition and position in the House of Täklä Haymanot.

This church training led to the Solomonid state. Years later, Täsfa Ṣeyon told his Roman colleagues that he had been a secretary for Gälawdéwos (Figure 2), suggesting that he served the royal family in an administrative or scribal role, possibly as a subordinate to the court historian, or *ṣähafé te'ezaz*, or the monastic keeper of the hours, or *aqqabé sä'at*.[36] The first office was eventually held by his superior Enbaqom.[37] Since Täsfa Ṣeyon left Ethiopia before the 1540 coronation of Gälawdéwos, he presumably joined the court during the prior reign of Lebnä Dengel, when the latter's son and heir was a minor. This possibility is raised by the variant orthography that Täsfa Ṣeyon consistently used for the emperor's name,[38] implying that his service perhaps preceded Gälawdéwos's period of social eminence. Yet the possibility of a more proximate relationship to the future emperor is suggested by the royal biographer of Gälawdéwos, who describes the latter's rigorous childhood church education, and the precedent of the chronicler of Emperor Bä'edä Maryam (1468–78), an ecclesiastic who served the royal family as a preceptor and intergenerational annalist.[39] Whatever its particulars, Täsfa Ṣeyon's position ensconced him within the immense apparatus of the itinerant royal court, or *kätäma*. In addition

---

[35] Derat, *Domaine*.

[36] Täsfa Ṣeyon to Pietro Paolo Gualtieri, Rome 17 September 1547, BI, MS D, V, 13, 252r: "ጸሐፊ ዘአጽናፍ ስገደ[ድ] በጺጋ አግዚአብሔር ገለ[ኣ]ውዴዎስ." See Online Appendix Item 2.

[37] Solomon Gebreyes, *Gälawdewos*, 50–54.

[38] *TN*, 113r; and Täsfa Ṣeyon to Pietro Paolo Gualtieri, Rome 17 September 1547, BI, MS D, V, 13, 252r: "ገለውዴዎስ," for "ገላውዴዎስ." See also Online Appendix Item 1.

[39] Perruchon, *Zar'a Yâ'eqôb*.

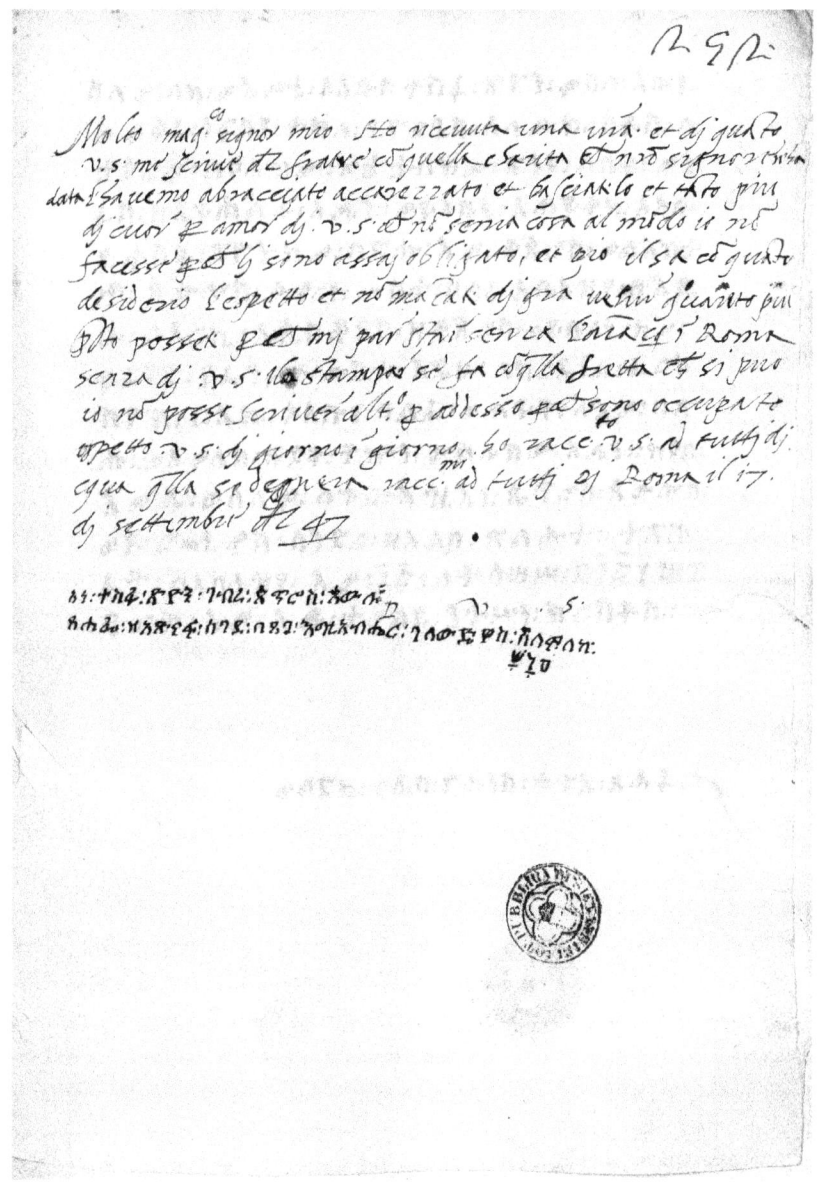

Figure 2 Täsfa Ṣeyon to Pietro Paolo Gualtieri, 17 September 1547, Rome, Biblioteca Comunale Intronati di Siena, ms. D V 13, cc. 252r (reprinted with permission of the Biblioteca Comunale degli Intronati, Istituzione del Comune di Siena)

to the emperor and royal family, this included the civil and military officials who comprised the royal council and central state administration, the *liqawent* who served as judges, advisors, and clerks, and the court pages drawn from the Christian and non-Christian populations of the realm.[40] At its apex, the *kätäma* numbered in the tens of thousands. Täsfa Ṣeyon thus counted among the religious elite who sustained Solomonid power.

This role placed him in a precarious position during the era's intertwined conflicts. In 1532, as war ravaged the highlands, the army of ʾAḥmad Grañ destroyed Däbrä Libanos and the community was dispersed, including *eççhägé* Enbaqom.[41] It was a calamity. Describing these events years later, Täsfa Ṣeyon lamented with great emotion the suffering of "my mother, Holy Ethiopia," who had been "crushed and weakened" by the invader:[42] "['Aḥmad Grañ] burnt our churches and our books and our offerings and defiled our churches and monasteries, by his perverse left hand."[43] As the Solomonid forces continued to battle the Adal invaders, the *liqawent* continued their fervid literary production, seeking to restore and defend the cultural patrimony of the Christian kingdom. It was a salvific project that left an impression on Täsfa Ṣeyon. Meanwhile, a number of monks and ecclesiastics attempted the arduous pilgrimage to Egypt and the Holy Land, turning to faith at a moment of collective trial. Some were successful; others turned back.[44] At some point in the early 1530s, Täsfa Ṣeyon followed their example and set out for Jerusalem, possibly because of the destruction of Däbrä Libanos.[45]

He reached the Holy Land before 1535, where he joined its small but venerable Ethiopian community (Figure 3). Pilgrims from the Horn had ventured to the Holy Land since late antiquity, arriving via a treacherous land route through Egypt and across the Sinai peninsula, with stops at the desert monasteries of al-Qūsīya (Qwesqwam), Wādī al-Naṭrūn (Asqéṭes), and Saint Catherine's of Mount Sinai (Däbrä Sina).[46] By the late fifteenth century, Ethiopians maintained several residences and places of worship in Jerusalem, most notably at Däbrä Šelṭan, on the roof of the Church of the Holy Sepulcher in the city's Christian quarter.[47] If few in number, they were relatively prominent: they received ambassadors from the Ethiopian emperors, dispatched a delegation to the Council of Florence (1439–49),[48] and led the city's public ceremony of the Holy Fire, or Redätä Berhan, celebrated with senior Armenian,

---

[40] Deresse Ayenachew, "Territorial Expansion." [41] Solomon Gebreyes, *Gälawdewos*, 234.
[42] *TN*, 113r. [43] *TN*, 100v. See Online Appendix Item 4. [44] Conti Rossini, "Pāwlos," 290.
[45] Ḥeruy Wäldä Śellasé, ፕዙማ; Nosnitsin, "Däbrä Libanos."
[46] Cerulli, *Etiopi in Palestina*, Vol. 2, 372; Kelly, "Ethiopian Diasporas."
[47] Tedeschi, "Dayr as-Sultan."
[48] The council was a continuation of the Council of Basel, which had been convened in 1431and continued in a rump form until 1449: Gill, *Council of Florence*.

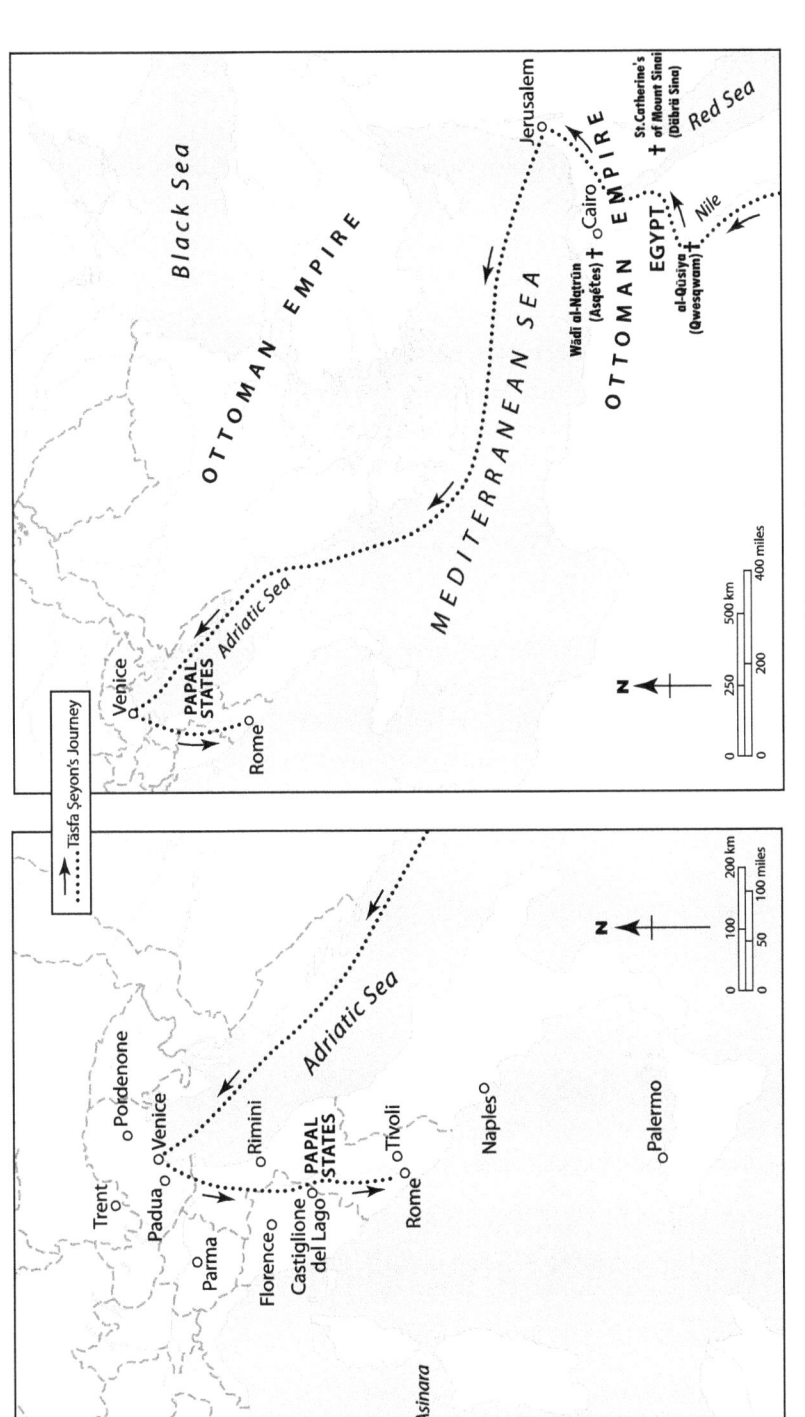

Figure 3 Täsfa Ṣeyon's itinerary (David McCutcheon)

Coptic, and Greek ecclesiastics outside the Church of the Holy Sepulcher.[49] But their position in Jerusalem was precarious. As one of the Holy City's many non-Muslim minorities, or *dhimmī*, they were subject to the changing dynamics of Muslim, Christian, and Jewish relations,[50] which deteriorated in the decades before Täsfa Ṣeyon's arrival. During the late Mamluk period, the city faced calls to enforce the legal restrictions on Christians, and one eminent *qāḍī* ordered the public execution of an Ethiopian Christian for blasphemy, apparently transgressing the will of the sultan with the sentence. His supporters burned the body of this unfortunate in the courtyard of the Church of the Holy Sepulcher.[51] The situation became more complex after the 1517 Ottoman conquest,[52] when the Ethiopians were obliged to accommodate themselves to the Ottoman system of managing intercommunal relations through religious authorities. In this, they were eventually subordinated to the Armenian Patriarchate of Jerusalem, the designated authority over the non-Greek Orthodox Christians of the Ottoman Arab provinces.[53] This arrangement exacerbated the Ethiopians' already-limited autonomy. It is thus unsurprising that the community declined in the early sixteenth century.[54]

We have few details about Täsfa Ṣeyon's stay in Jerusalem. A hint of his journey comes from the records of the Ethiopian community of Qwesqwam, on the upper Nile in Egypt. A marginal annotation in one of its Ge'ez manuscripts explains that a sixteenth-century visitor named Täsfa Ṣeyon donated a cow to the community, in honor of the Virgin Mary.[55] Though the reference is uncertain, it suggests the wealthy origins later described by Täsfa Ṣeyon's Roman contemporaries. A further glimpse of his travels appeared years later, when he and the Ethiopians of Rome recalled the difficult journey from Ethiopia to Jerusalem:

> The pilgrims ... traveled [through] the sand, the desert, [over] many snakes; [they] suffered from hunger and thirst; burned by the heat of the sun; and above all, they were tormented by the Ishmaelites, the children of Hagar [i.e., the Muslims of Egypt]; out of the love for Christ and the Holy Land of Jerusalem, the place of His suffering, crucifixion, death, burial, and resurrection [from] among the dead [Figure 4].[56]

There are no known traces of Täsfa Ṣeyon's time among the Ethiopians of Ottoman Jerusalem. From his later writings, we only know that he spent a few

---

[49] *EA*, Vol. 4, 353–54.
[50] Sharkey, *Muslims, Christians, and Jews*; Makdisi, *Age of Coexistence*.
[51] Little, "Mamlūk Jerusalem," 75–76.   [52] Ze'evi, *Ottoman Century*.
[53] Bardakjian, "Armenian Patriarchate."
[54] Cerulli, *Etiopi in Palestina*, Vol. 1, xli–xlv; Tedeschi, "Dayr as-Sultan."
[55] BAV, Vat. Et. 32, 104r.   [56] BAV, Vat. Et. 66, 56r. See Online Appendix Item 1.

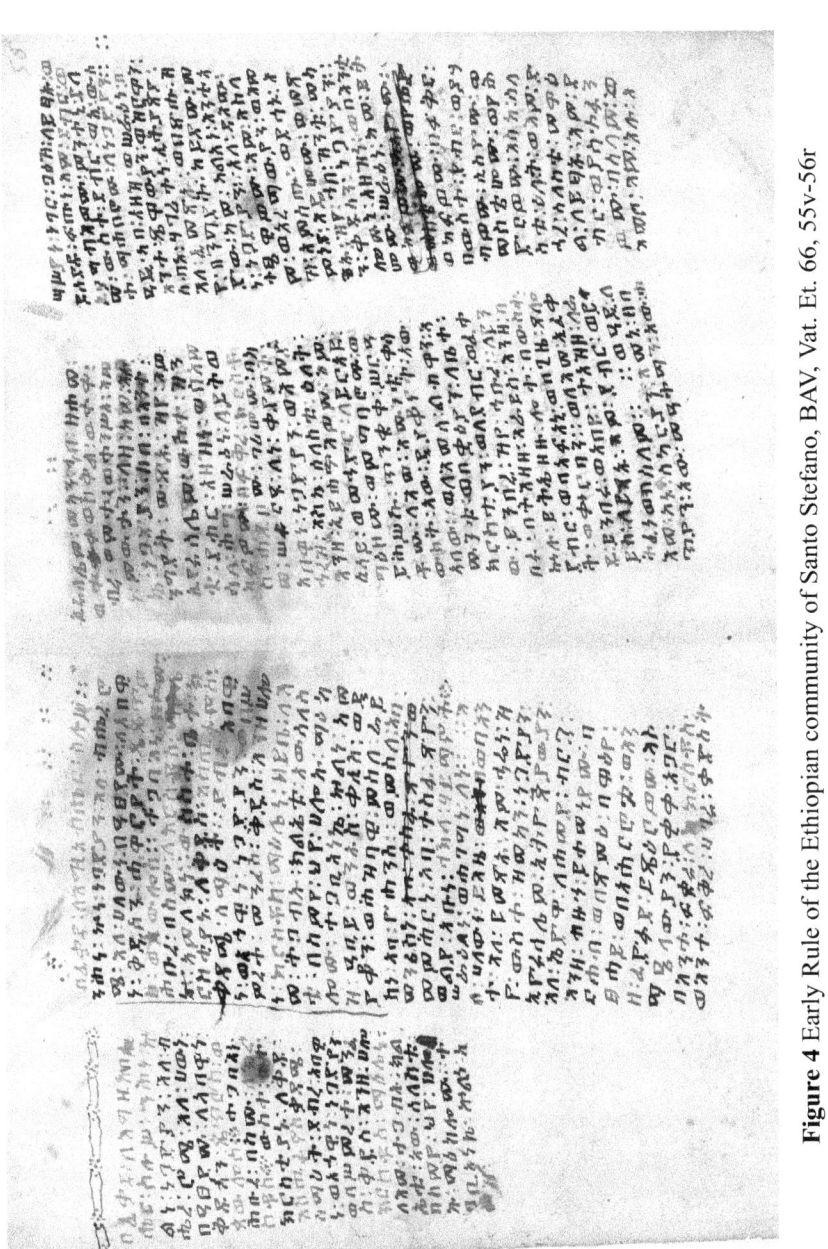

Figure 4 Early Rule of the Ethiopian community of Santo Stefano, BAV, Vat. Et. 66, 55v–56r

years in the Holy Land, presumably at Däbrä Selṭan. At some point in the mid-1530s, he boarded a ship for the Italian peninsula. His final destination was Rome, the resplendent capital of the Papal States.

The Other Holy Land

By the sixteenth century, Rome was the most cosmopolitan city of Latin Europe. As the center of global Catholicism, it hosted growing numbers of pilgrims, students, ecclesiastics, monks, and missionaries from throughout the Catholic world and beyond. For many observers, the cultural and linguistic diversity of these *nationes*, or resident non-Italian communities, exemplified the triumph of the faith and splendor of the universal church, of which Rome was the sacred capital and magnificent theater.[57] While many immigrants obtained accommodation and support networks through employment, the more established foreign Catholic communities also enjoyed confraternities, designated churches, and national colleges and seminaries for their clergy, through which they displayed their particularity within the universal.[58] These preeminent *nationes* were joined by smaller populations of more eclectic origins, including a heterogenous array of non-Catholic strangers[59] and religious minorities. These included Italian and non-Italian Protestants and Jews, enslaved Muslims from Africa and the Middle East, and so-called Eastern Christians from throughout the Mediterranean.

This last group included several distinct populations of Orthodox Christians. The most numerous were the Armenians, who were among the most prosperous minorities in Rome through their connection to a far-flung global trade diaspora.[60] They were joined by Greeks from throughout the Levant, including many refugees from the 1453 Ottoman conquest of Constantinople, as well as Maronites from present-day Lebanon, who followed a branch of the Syriac Orthodox Church in communion with Rome.[61] In the later sixteenth century, the Vatican institutionalized its relationship with these Eastern Christian *nationes* by establishing the Armenian Church of Santa Maria Egiziaca (1566),[62] the Pontifical Greek College (1577),[63] and the Pontifical Maronite College (1584), thereby seeking to control the diasporic communities and advance the spread of Catholicism in the Middle East (Figure 5).[64] This ecclesiastic surveillance intensified after the Roman Inquisition targeted the city's religious minorities, including unconverted Eastern Christians.[65]

---

[57] Coneys Wainwright and Michelson, "Introduction," 1–12; Esche-Ramshorn, "Pilgrim Centre," 173.
[58] Girard and Pizzorusso, "Maronite College," 176.   [59] Simmel, "Stranger."
[60] Santus, "Wandering Lives."   [61] Kennerley, *Rome and the Maronites*, 9.
[62] Santus, "Pellegrini."   [63] Santus, "Presenza greca," 194–95.
[64] Fosi, "Nationes," 389; Santus, "Pellegrini orientali."   [65] Santus, "Wandering Lives."

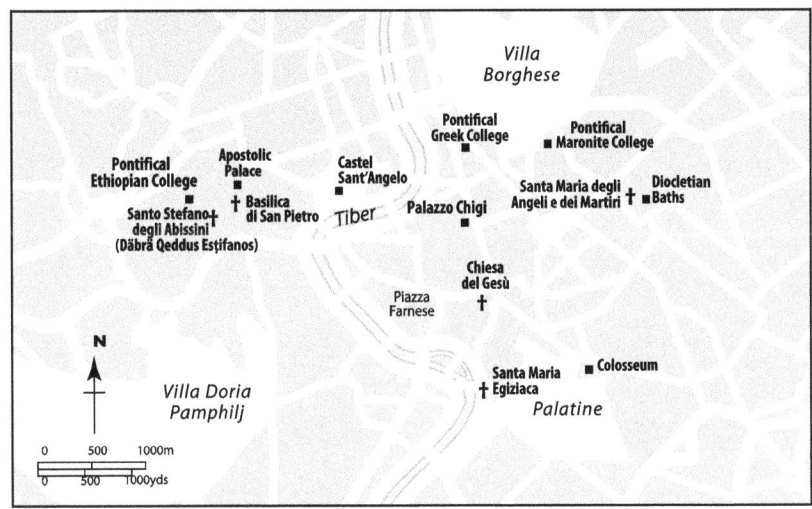

Figure 5 Täsfa Ṣeyon's Rome (David McCutcheon)

By the early sixteenth century, Rome was also home to a growing Ethiopian community. It was centered at Santo Stefano Maggiore, one of four church-cum-monasteries within the Vatican walls owned by the Chapter of Saint Peter and used by basilica personnel (Figure 6). Dedicated to Saint Stephen of Jerusalem (ca. 5–34), the protomartyr of Christianity, the church and its residential annex were built under Pope Leo I (440–461).[66] At some point in the late fifteenth century, Santo Stefano began to be occupied by Ethiopian pilgrims,[67] at which time it became known as Santo Stefano degli Abissini, using the European exonym "Abyssinian" to describe the highland Christians of present-day Ethiopia and Eritrea. In a reflection of the prevailing European geographic confusion with respect to Africa, the complex was also known as Santo Stefano degli Indiani, dei Mori, and degli Egiziani, employing the era's other common terms for Ethiopians ("Indians" and "Moors"), and additionally mistaking them for another poorly understood Eastern Christian community ("Egyptians," meaning Coptic Orthodox Christians).[68]

When Täsfa Ṣeyon arrived in the 1530s, Santo Stefano had become a distinct Ethiopian diasporic space at the heart of Latin Christendom. This development is epitomized by its Ge'ez, Amharic, and Tigrinya name: Däbrä Qeddus Esṭifanos,

---

[66] Mauro da Leonessa, *Santo Stefano*, 2, 41; Proverbio, "Santo Stefano," 54; Raineri and Delsere, *S. Stefano dei Mori*.
[67] On the timing and nature of Santo Stefano's association with the Ethiopian community, see Kelly, *Translating Faith*, 38–46.
[68] Hamilton, *Copts and the West*.

Figure 6 View of Santo Stefano from Giuseppe Vasi, *Raccolta delle piú belle vedute antiche, e moderne di Roma* (Rome: 1803) (Photo by the author)

lit. "Mount of Saint Stephen." This moniker suggests a specific institutional identity rooted in Ethiopian monastic norms. Literally, the word *däbr* refers to a hill, mountain, or extremely high location, and it is a common component of toponyms throughout Ethiopia and Eritrea. Within the Ethiopian monastic tradition, *däbr* is more specifically employed in the names of important monasteries and churches, such as Däbrä Libanos in Shäwa, Däbrä Ḥayq in Amhara, and Däbrä Dammo and Däbrä Abbay in Tegray. In addition to sustaining monastic residents, *däbr*s are also dedicated to community worship, education, and evangelism, and for this reason, they maintain teachers, liturgical musicians, and church scholars. Their leaders sometimes occupied important external ecclesiastic and court appointments. As institutions that served monastics as well as the wider community (*yädäbr ḥezb*, lit. "people of the *däbr*"), they are distinct from rural parish churches (*gäṭär*), which are maintained by the local community and its ecclesiastics, as well as remote monasteries (*gädam*), which are focused on ascetic religious seclusion. More broadly, *däbr*s are perceived by the faithful as holy places of immense spiritual and intellectual significance: they are sites of miraculous intercession, extreme self-denial, and deep religious learning, and are sometimes imagined as exemplars of the historical fortunes of Ethiopian Christianity.[69] By christening Santo Stefano a *däbr*, the Ethiopians of Rome signaled their precise understanding of its institutional identity: Däbrä Qeddus

---

[69] *EA* Vol. 3: 987–993; Kindeneh Endeg Mihretie, "Waldəba."

Estifanos was dedicated to maintaining a community of Ethiopian monastics, ecclesiastics, and lay people while sustaining the steady flow of travelers to the shrines of Saints Peter and Paul. In a material gesture to this role, the community obtained three clay trivet stones, or *gulecha*, to prepare traditional Ethiopian food, as well as five wooden kegs for brewing *tej*, or honey wine, and *berz*, a lightly fermented high caloric beverage that is well-suited to the weary traveler.[70] Santo Stefano was an Orthodox monastery and the "safe abode of the Ethiopian pilgrims" in the Roman Holy Land.[71]

In the early sixteenth century, it developed several institutional features befitting this role. Most conspicuously, the community consecrated its *tabot*, or altar ark and tablets, to Saint Stephen, who thereby became its patron saint and collective intercessor.[72] This was a foundational moment. In the Ethiopian Orthodox tradition, a church cannot exist without a *tabot*: it is the dwelling relic of the Holy Spirit, and is consecrated to the angel, saint, or martyr for whom the church is named, through which process it becomes the physical presence of its namesake and the instrument for conveying the prayers of the faithful. Its theft, desecration, or destruction is considered disastrous.[73] The presence of a consecrated *tabot* at Santo Stefano indicates the community's rigorous adherence to Ethiopian Orthodox norms, transforming a Vatican Catholic Church into an Ethiopian place of worship. As a ritual expression of this fact, the community also maintained the crosses, incense burners, eucharistic vessels, and sacerdotal vestments required by the Ethiopian mass, including those required by the Feast of the Epiphany, or Ṭemqät, as well as the annual *tabot* exaltation for the feast of its patron saint, or *negś*, which both involve processions outside the church.[74] Tellingly, the community celebrated the Feast of Saint Stephen in accordance with the Ethiopian religious calendar, and not its Catholic counterpart, and an announcement of this fact in an eighteenth-century Ge'ez collection of saints' lives appears to be the earliest exogenous reference to Santo Stefano in Ethiopian literature.[75] The community's public worship intrigued more than one early sixteenth-century observer.[76]

Beyond the *tabot*, the residents of Santo Stefano also structured their community through Ethiopian monastic models. Its abbot or head held the title *rayes*, following the distinctive Arabic-derived terminology used by the Ethiopian diaspora communities in Jerusalem and Qwesqwam.[77] In Rome,

---

[70] BAV, Vat. Et. 66, 2r. See Online Appendix Item 1.
[71] BAV, R.I.IV 2218, 229r: "መንደረ ነጋድያን ኢትዮጵያውያን"; see also BAV, Vat. Et. 66, 57v.
[72] BAV, Vat. Et. 66, 2v.   [73] Getatchew Haile, "Tabot."   [74] BAV, Vat. Et. 66, 2r.
[75] BL, Or. 662, 20r.
[76] Potken and Tomas Wäldä Samu'él, *Psalterium*, 1v; Ramusio, *Navigationi*, 1v.
[77] Cerulli, *Etiopi in Palestina*, Vol. 2, 355–68.

the *rayes* was appointed by the community and wielded considerable power within it, though they were not the primary intermediary with respect to its relations with the outside world. This function fell to the *mäggabi*, or administrator/steward, an office found at the other diaspora monasteries as well as in a range of monastic, ecclesiastic, and secular settings in Ethiopia. In Rome, the *mäggabi* was the treasurer and provisioner of the community, responsible for managing its communal property, donations, and expenses, and seems to have been subordinate in these functions to the *rayes*. A third office was the teacher, or *mämher*, a position that does not seem to have existed at the other diaspora monasteries, but was a title of learning and authority at Ethiopian monasteries like Däbrä Libanos.[78] These three officials served the wider community of the *däbr*, who were divided between temporary and permanent members, and who were collectively known as "the pilgrims of Däbrä Qeddus Estifanos at the Sepulcher of Peter and Paul." They were in turn one aspect of the broader diaspora of "pilgrims who are in the land of foreigners."[79]

In several respects, though, the institutional features of Santo Stefano diverged from Ethiopian monastic norms, as the community accommodated itself to its distinctive diasporic setting. One unusual situation developed in the mid-sixteenth century, when the *mäggabi* of Santo Stefano was Pietro Paolo Gualtieri (1501–72), a lay scholar from Arezzo who studied Ge'ez at Santo Stefano and who was deeply involved in curial relations with Eastern Christians, such that the Ethiopians celebrated him as "a close friend of the pilgrims."[80] We find no precedent for a non-Orthodox – let alone a Catholic – holding such a position in an Ethiopian monastery, diasporic or otherwise. Another distinctive aspect of Santo Stefano was the fact that it welcomed lay Ethiopian guests, whether these were pilgrims or non-religious travelers. These visitors were permitted to stay at the residence and petition to join its permanent community, subject to the decision of the other residents. The *däbr* was thus a refuge and sanctuary for the community of the faithful far from home, not just a place of religious learning and seclusion. This institutional role distinguished Santo Stefano from the other diasporic monasteries, which seem to have been reserved for monastics and ecclesiastics, unlike their *däbr* counterparts in Ethiopia.

Even more unusual was Santo Stefano's synthetic and relatively accommodating monastic culture. For more than a century, the Ethiopian church had been

---

[78] Getatchew Haile, "Däbrä Libanos."
[79] BAV, Vat. Et. 66, 2v: "ነጋድያን በደብረ ቅዳስ እስጢፋኖስ በዝጎረ ጴጥሮስ ወጳውሎስ"
[80] BAV, R.I.IV 2218, 229v, 233r: "መፍቀሬ"; *TN*, 176v, 226v.

divided by a controversy concerning Sabbath observance.[81] In this, the heterodox House of Ēwosṭatēwos embraced the Saturday "First Sabbath," clashing with the House of Däbrä Libanos and the remainder of the church, which maintained the Alexandrine position favoring the Sunday "Christian Sabbath" and rejecting the Saturday alternative as Judaic. These controversies divided the religious of Ethiopia into clashing northern and southern factions until the 1449 Council of Däbrä Meṭmaq, where Emperor Zär'a Ya'eqob forced the adoption of two Sabbaths over the objections of the Coptic metropolitan and Däbrä Libanos *liqawent*,[82] as a compromise aimed at unifying the church and kingdom. When Santo Stefano was established nearly a century later, this forced reconciliation was further compounded by the shared crisis of the Adal invasion, which destroyed monasteries without regard for their doctrinal positions. For the children of Ēwosṭatēwos and Däbrä Libanos alike, it was a time of collective suffering, survival, and recovery.

In Rome, the assembled disciples of these clashing monastic lines lived in apparent harmony. The disputes of home seem to have been ignored abroad, despite the occasional calls for internal unity within the Ge'ez records of the community. This point is suggested by the fact that the residents of Santo Stefano publicly acknowledged their monastic affiliations, describing themselves as the children of the founding father of their respective monastic tradition, and in some cases seemingly adopting titles from their home monasteries, such as *mämher*, or teacher; *däbtära*, or lay ecclesiastic; *liqä diyaqonat*, or archdeacon; and *liqä kahenat*, or archpriest.[83] Even more unusually, the leaders of the community represented both monastic houses, even though Däbrä Libanos seem to have predominated. This intellectual heterogeneity suggests that Sabbath observance was not a source of conflict between the rival houses at Santo Stefano, even as the residents self-identified through the dogmatic positions of monastic lineage. We therefore speculate that the community observed both Sabbaths, in keeping with the Däbrä Meṭmaq edict.[84] In this, the situation at Santo Stefano diverged substantially from the Catholic observation.

By the time Täsfa Seyon arrived, community relations were governed by an established rule, or *serä'atä bētä krestyan*.[85] This rule was elaborated by the residents over several decades, and was preserved in two Ge'ez manuscripts as well as in the final pages of a printed Ge'ez New Testament, where it appears in

---

[81] Taddesse Tamrat, *Church and State*; Adankpo-Labadie, *Moines, saints et hérétiques*.
[82] Getatchew Haile, "Mika'el and Gäbrə'el."   [83] BAV, Vat. Et. 66, 2r, 54r, 56r, 65r.
[84] Getatchew Haile, "Mika'el and Gäbrə'el," 73–78.   [85] "Rule of the church."

Ge'ez as well as Latin.[86] All three of these texts were maintained in the Santo Stefano library, a shared collection of Ge'ez codices and printed books that was sustained by donations and purchases from the community.[87] The earliest forms of the community rule were oral, originating with pilgrim praxis and likely first articulated at the turn of the sixteenth century. Between 1528 and 1551, the community established more formal regulations.[88] Among these was the stipulation that visitors to Santo Stefano would be "received with the love of Christ" and granted food and lodging for three days, after which time they could petition to stay. These requests were evaluated by the permanent members of the community. The residents of the *däbr* were also bound to "live [according] to the orders of the *rayes*," and obey its rules "through their [good] words, and during the prayers and communion." Misconduct for infractions like quarrelsomeness, drunkenness, carrying weapons, or slandering members as Muslims, Jews, or hyenas were punished by fines or permanent expulsion.[89] Special provision was made for Ethiopian visitors who had been "captured by the Muslims and unbelievers": they too would receive sanctuary for three days.[90] In comparison with monastic rules in Ethiopia, the Santo Stefano rule was less focused on details of worship and more concerned with accommodating newcomers and establishing standards of interpersonal behavior. In short, it confronted the distinctive challenges of diasporic life.

As the rule suggests, Santo Stefano was not without its conflicts. Its community annal, a Ge'ez manuscript preserved today as Vat. Et. 66 at the Biblioteca Apostolica Vaticana, occasionally describes specific moments of challenge, as documents of history and warnings to future residents. Some of these incidents involved minor property and financial disputes.[91] A more serious episode involved a resident named Ḫalib who killed someone and was expelled from the community. After going away to "another country," he returned to Santo Stefano and did "wickedness": robbing the residents, beating a *däbtära*, and stealing the *tabot* cloth, the valuable cover of the community's most sacred object. He was excommunicated for these crimes, and the community annalist warned that anyone who allowed his return would be cursed by "the sword of words" of Saints Peter and Paul, alluding to Ephesians 6:17.[92] Another dramatic dispute involved *rayes* Enqwä Maryam of Cyprus, who in 1528–29 denounced the residents to a Vatican official, who in turn sanctioned the community by ending its food allotment. Enqwä Maryam accused them of violating their vow

---

[86] BAV, Vat. Et. 29 and 66; *TN* in BAV, R.I.IV 2218, 227–34.
[87] Adankpo-Labadie, *Moines, saints et hérétiques*.   [88] BAV, Vat. Et. 66, 65r.
[89] BAV, Vat. Et. 66, 67r.   [90] BAV, Vat. Et. 66, 56r.   [91] BAV, Vat. Et. 66, 2v.
[92] BAV, Vat. Et. 66, 2v. For a comprehensive account of the residents of Santo Stefano, see Kelly, *Translating Faith*, esp. 301–23.

of celibacy, alleging they were "fornicators with women" and "male with a male." The scandal became known "all over [the city] of Rome," and after the residents petitioned Pope Clement VII (1523–34), the *rayes* was then expelled from the *däbr*.[93] The entire affair exposed the growing links between the Ethiopian community and the personalities and institutions of their adopted home.

Myths, Lies, and Truths

This was the world that greeted Täsfa Ṣeyon. We do not know precisely when he arrived in Rome. Years later, he simply called the city the ideal "resting place for my body and soul," in that it was the final abode of Saints Peter and Paul and the founders of the early church.[94] The community annal, meanwhile, first mentions his presence at the *däbr* in a 1551 note about his contribution to the community rule, wherein he is identified with the honorific "our teacher."[95] The earliest notice of his presence in Rome instead derives from his involvement in a 1536 controversy that spread his name far beyond the quiet world of Santo Stefano.

The affair involved the case of João Bermudes (1491–1570), the former surgeon of the 1520 Portuguese mission to Lebnä Dengel. After reaching the Horn, Bermudes had remained in the warring Ethiopian highlands until the 1530s, when he claimed that Lebnä Dengel returned him to Europe on a double mission to Rome and Lisbon, offering the emperor's obedience to the pontiff and seeking military support from João III. In 1536, Bermudes arrived in Rome, where he made an astonishing claim. In addition to asserting his credentials as the representative of Lebnä Dengel, he alleged that *abunä* Marqos (nd–1529/30), the dying Egyptian metropolitan, had named him as his ecclesiastic successor.[96] In short, Bermudes alleged that a Portuguese lay Catholic with no training or experience was now head of the Ethiopian Orthodox Church. This was preposterous: since its inception, the non-autocephalous Ethiopian church had been headed by a Coptic bishop appointed by the Patriarch of Alexandria in consultation with the residents of Saint Anthony's monastery in Egypt. This appointed metropolitan, or *abun*, had never named his own successor.

These details transcended the limits of Vatican knowledge. At that time, the European understanding of Ethiopia was intertwined with the enduring myth of Prester John. This imagination had emerged in the twelfth century, when an apocryphal letter from a mysterious sovereign circulated throughout Europe. It described the pious ruler of a distant but mighty kingdom through an exoticist

---

[93] BAV, Vat. Et. 66, 65v–66r. [94] *TN*, 225r. [95] BAV, Vat. Et. 66, 56r.
[96] Whiteway, *Expedition to Abyssinia*, 129–30.

pastiche of ancient texts, medieval legends, and contemporary rumor, suggesting a European fabulist perhaps authored the original letter, possibly as an allegory of the perfect Christian king.[97] Whatever its origins, the document acquired a life of its own, and in the estimation of European Christendom, Prester John seemed a potential game-changing ally in the ongoing crusade against the Islamic world.

But where was his kingdom, exactly? The earliest twelfth-century versions of the myth located it in East Asia, a region then barely understood by most Europeans. Over the ensuing centuries, Prester John's presumed home was repeatedly relocated across Asia and the Horn of Africa, then conceived as part of continental Asia, or the Indies.[98] An Ethiopian connection first emerged in the fourteenth century, and grew stronger as visitors from the Christian kingdom began to arrive in Europe, where their surprised hosts associated them with the mythic ruler.[99] The promise of an Ethiopian Prester John eventually captivated the papacy as well as European monarchs like King Alfonso V of Aragon (1396–1458), who proved eager to forge an anti-Muslim alliance with a distant co-religionist.[100] In the early fifteenth century, the Portuguese House of Avis sponsored the reconnaissance of Atlantic Africa, seeking the fabled potentate as well as commerce and a maritime route to India,[101] and in 1497, King João II (1455–95) dispatched Vasco da Gama (1460–1524) to the Indian Ocean, in part to find the elusive Prester John.[102] After countless failed efforts, in 1514 an Ethiopian emissary unexpectedly arrived at the court of King Manuel I (1495–1521). Believing himself now in direct communication with the long-sought ruler, the Portuguese monarch sent a delegation to Ethiopia, which in 1520 reached Lebnä Dengel. When the news returned to Europe, the medieval quest for Prester John seemed finally fulfilled, compounding the gravity of the European discovery of the Americas. This epochal conjuncture framed the shocking 1536 story of Bermudes.

This heady context led the curia to summon Täsfa Ṣeyon. The Jesuit Alfonso Salmeron (1515–85) described the ensuing audience: "A Portuguese man [Bermudes] had come from Prester John's India [Ethiopia] [with] letters to Rome, for the Pope. Friar Pedro [Täsfa Ṣeyon], who is from there, was asked to read them and so was a priest [Yoḥannes of Cyprus] who is with Cardinal Theatino [Gian Pietro Carafa]."[103] It would seem that Täsfa Ṣeyon was tasked with translating the surgeon's letters from the emperor. Given his distinction as

---

[97] Beckingham and Hamilton, *Prester John*. [98] Relaño, *Shaping of Africa*.
[99] Taylor, "Imaginary King," 132–34. [100] Salvadore, *Prester John*, 36–53.
[101] Newitt, *Portuguese Overseas Expansion*. [102] Subrahmanyam, *Da Gama*.
[103] Alfonso Salmeron to Ignatius of Loyola, Trent, October 1546, in Salmeron, *Epistolae*, Vol. 1, 33–36.

one of the most learned residents of Santo Stefano, he was likely asked to assess Bermudes's claims and explain the workings of the Ethiopian Orthodox Church, then obscure to Europeans. As an alumnus of Däbrä Libanos and Lebnä Dengel's court, Täsfa Ṣeyon would have found it easy to persuade the surely skeptical curia to reject Bermudes's bid for ecclesiastic power – even if the latter would go on to falsely boast that Paul III appointed him not only *abun* of Ethiopia but also "Patriarch and Pontifex" of Alexandria.[104] In the process, Täsfa Ṣeyon helped expose a prominent and potentially compromising fraud, thereby becoming the resident Vatican expert on Ethiopia and the Horn. The stage was now set for an unprecedented career.

3 The *mämher* of Rome

In 1544, the maverick French orientalist Guillaume Postel (1510–81) arrived in Rome.[105] He was on a mission. Following a divine voice and imagining himself a scholar-prophet, he had spent years reconstructing the primordial language of God, which he believed would be the unifying instrument for a universal Abrahamic religion and its emerging earthly kingdom.[106] After starting with Greek and Latin philology, this esoteric undertaking led him to study Hebrew and Kabbalah in Paris, and Arabic, Turkish, and the Quran in Constantinople. He then published a comparative study of writing systems (1537), the first printed Arabic grammar (1538), a history of languages (1538), and a missiological concordance of Islam, Christianity, and Judaism (1544), the last featuring original Hebrew and Arabic translations. In 1539, these achievements won Postel the first Arabic professorship at the Collège Royal, the future Collège de France. Yet despite his politic conviction that the French crown would lead his world monarchy, he soon alienated King Francis I (1515–47), and in 1544, he abandoned the academy and fled to Rome, where he joined the newly established Society of Jesus. He was expelled after one year.

Now alone in Rome, Postel returned to his research. Increasingly enamored by Eastern Christian languages and literature, he visited the Ethiopian community at Santo Stefano, where he met Täsfa Ṣeyon.[107] The two discussed the Book of Enoch, an ancient Hebrew text then nearly unknown to Europeans,[108] but preserved via Ge'ez translation within the canon of the Ethiopian Orthodox Church.[109] Postel found the *mämher* deeply knowledgeable about the text and

---

[104] Whiteway, *Expedition to Abyssinia*, 130.
[105] Kuntz, *Postel*; Petry, *Mystical Theology*; Wilkinson, *Orientalism*.
[106] Wheeler, "Primordial Origins." [107] BL, Sloane Ms. 1411, 124v.
[108] Erho and Stuckenbruck, "Ethiopic Enoch." [109] Daniel Assefa, "Uriel."

its meaning, later describing him as "a man of notable piety."[110] Their dialogue convinced Postel that Enoch – which recounts the angelic journeys of an antediluvian patriarch – was a pre-Mosaic prophetic transmission of "the order of nature" and the esoteric key to all scripture, for which reason, he averred, it was considered "a sacred authority" by "the Church of Prester John."[111] Shortly after this encounter, in 1547, Postel also became convinced that a Venetian mystic named Mother Joanna was a messianic "New Eve," and after becoming her disciple, he spent the remainder of his life elaborating the heretical eschatology of her new epoch, based in part on his unique understanding of Enoch. Along the way, he incorporated Ethiopia into his universal imaginary, asserting its residents were "the most perfect Christians in the world."[112] In 1555, he was finally imprisoned by the Inquisition, and he spent his last decades in a lunatic asylum. Today, Postel is considered an idiosyncratic but pioneering student of comparative philology and Semitic linguistics.[113] He was the first orientalist.[114]

Postel's encounter with Täsfa Ṣeyon is doubly illustrative. On the one hand, it exemplifies the distinct concerns of early modern orientalism and the paradigm of *philologia sacra*. Postel saw the study of ancient and living Semitic languages as a means of deepening Christian understanding, and for this reason, his research focused on the Holy Land, and not an expansive Asian orient.[115] In this, he typified the early modern orientalist fusion of a new dedication to the study of Eastern languages and texts with an older conviction that this enterprise would further the universal crusade against the Islamic world. The command of oriental languages was thus soteriological, in that it would further the conversion of Muslims and the denigration of their faith. With respect to Ethiopia, these concerns produced a corresponding orientalist fixation on Prester John, Eastern Christianity, and the Ge'ez Bible, spanning myth, doctrine, and text.

On the other hand, Postel's consultation at Santo Stefano suggests the foundational contribution of diasporic African and Asian intellectuals to the development of European orientalist learning. They were librarians, copyists, advisors, teachers, translators, editors, and authors, and in these varied roles

---

[110] BL, Sloane Ms. 1411, 124v, with Täsfa Ṣeyon's description of the Enochian Garden of Eden on 125r.
[111] BL, Sloane Ms. 1411, 124v.
[112] Postel, *Histoires orientales*, 47; and more generally, Postel, *Candélabre de Moyse*, 29, n. 61.
[113] Contini, "Linguistica semitica." He was additionally an early European defender of the antiquity of Indian literature: App, *Orientalism*.
[114] Febvre, *Problem of Unbelief*, 107–22; Lockman, *Contending Visions*, 44–45; Baghdiantz-McCabe, *Orientalism*, 15–36.
[115] Said, *Orientalism*, 51.

they shaped and tried to shape European knowledge of their homes in highly politicized contexts.[116] They met and taught their European counterparts, facilitated the printing of non-European texts, addressed the representation of their societies and religions, intervened in interconfessional controversies, and in some cases faced sanctions for their faith and views. In these respects, they were metropolitan analogues to the broader network of extra-European imperial intermediaries who shaped the production and circulation of Western knowledge about the wider world. Taking this intellectual dialectic as its point of departure, this chapter reconstructs Täsfa Ṣeyon's singular contribution to the sixteenth-century European understanding of Ethiopia.

The Birth of African Studies

This new understanding emerged from the contacts of the preceding century. As Iberian mariners traversed the Atlantic, circumnavigated the African continent, and entered the Indian Ocean, Ethiopian travelers ventured to Mediterranean Europe. In conversations with their hosts, they presented themselves as the subjects of a pious but powerful Christian kingdom beyond the Muslim world, seemingly confirming the European image of Prester John. Their testimony sharpened the European geographic understanding of the Horn of Africa. In Venice, where the city's maritime trade network brought Ethiopians from the Levant, these reports informed the *Iter de Venetiis ad Indiam* (1402), an anonymous itinerary that described the route to Prester John's kingdom alongside an Amharic-Italian lexicon, the first European dictionary of an African language.[117] Decades later, the cartographer Fra Mauro Camaldolese (nd–1459) used testimony from the Ethiopian delegates to the Council of Florence to produce the *Mappamundi* (ca. 1450), which depicted Africa and especially the Horn in unprecedented detail.[118] This work was continued by geographer Alessandro Zorzi (ca. 1470–ca. 1538), whose early sixteenth-century compendium described pilgrimage routes from Ethiopia to Egypt and the Holy Land.[119] Complimentary works emerged elsewhere in the Italian peninsula. In Naples, the Dominican Pietro Ranzano (1428–92) interviewed an Ethiopian delegation to Alfonso V and presented the result in his *Annales Omnium Temporum* (1470s),[120] while in Tuscany, Poggio Bracciolini (1380–1459) met the Ethiopian delegation to the Council of Florence and described

---

[116] Hamilton, "Egyptian Traveller"; Ghobrial, "Archive of Orientalism"; Ghobrial, "Eastern Christians"; Girard, "Eastern Scholar"; Zemon Davis, *Trickster Travels*.
[117] Jorga, "Cenni."   [118] Falchetta, *Fra Mauro*, 201.
[119] BNCF Banco Rari 236, 28r–58v; Crawford, *Ethiopian Itineraries*.
[120] Ranzano, "Annales Omnium Temporum," BCP Man. 3Qq C 55, 91r-95v; Salvadore, *Prester John*, 45–47.

their home in his *De varietate fortunae* (1447).[121] He was in turn likely interviewed by the creator of the *Egyptus novelo* map (ca. 1454), which featured accurate toponyms for the Upper Nile Valley.[122] Collectively, these fifteenth- and early sixteenth-century works comprise a protean Ethiopianist library, the first corpus of European knowledge dedicated to an African society beyond the Sahara.

These Italian geographies and histories were products of chance, curiosity, and personal initiative. Their creators were scholars with a general interest in the non-European world, who seized opportunities to acquire rare but potentially useful information from transiting Ethiopians. Their basis was oral testimony. However, by the early sixteenth-century the tiny field of Ethiopianist research developed a new structure, attracting scholars with specialized and comparative interests in Eastern Christian languages, texts, and churches, buttressed by the institutionalized Ethiopian diasporic presence in Rome. This transformation coincided with the burgeoning European interest in the newly discovered societies of Asia and the Americas. Together, these developments re-situated Ethiopia-focused scholarship within the nascent field of early modern orientalism, the research agenda of *philologia sacra*, and the adjacent field of world historiography.

This shift is exemplified by the 1513 edition of the Ethiopian Psalter, or *Dawit*.[123] It is the first printed text in an African language, predating the Arabic Book of Hours by one year. As a multilingual work produced for both Ethiopian and European readers, the Psalter illuminates the changing dynamics of orientalist knowledge production and the agency of diasporic intellectuals therein. At that time, Santo Stefano was home to approximately thirty Ethiopian pilgrims.[124] In 1511, they intrigued Johannes Potken (1470–1524/5), a papal secretary from Cologne who became curious about their language, which he misidentified as Chaldean, or Aramaic.[125] He decided to study Ge'ez with Tomas Wäldä Samu'él, a monk from Waldebba then residing at Santo Stefano,[126] and in October 1511, Potken borrowed a manuscript of the Ge'ez Psalms from the Vatican Library, obtained from a 1481 Ethiopian delegation.[127] Two years later, he and Tomas published a print edition of the text with the Silber brothers of Rome.[128] Following Ethiopian convention, it contains the Ge'ez Book of Psalms, Song of Solomon, and collected songs and prayers, replicating in print the scribal features of the base manuscript.

---

[121] Tedeschi, "Bracciolini." [122] Mannoni, *Carta italiana*.
[123] Kelly, *Translating Faith*, 117–29; Lefevre, "Potken"; Raineri, "Studi etiopici," 118–23.
[124] Mauro da Leonessa, *Santo Stefano*, 187–89. [125] Kelly, "Curious Case."
[126] Potken and Tomas Wäldä Samu'él, *Psalterium*.
[127] BAV, Vat. Et. 20; BAV, Vat. Lat. 3966, 48r; Salvadore, *Prester John*, 68–75; *EA*, Vol. 5, 284–6. Cf. Krebs, *Ethiopian Kingship*, 122–39.
[128] Barberi, "Libri e stampatori," 222.

This was a watershed achievement. The work features the first printed autobiographical statement by an African author, provided as an interpolated Ge'ez leaf, and added to the volume shortly before printing, possibly unbeknownst to Potken:

> This *Dawit* [Psalms of David] was printed in the city of Rome by Johannes Potken, German and elder of the Church of Saint George of the city of Cologne of Germany, and with him, I Tomas Wäldä Samu'él, monk and pilgrim of Jerusalem, on the seventh of the month of Hamlé, the year of our Lord Jesus Christ, son of God and the Virgin Mary, 1513 Amen.[129]

As this attestation suggests, the project cast *abba* Tomas in a new intellectual role. Over the preceding century, diasporic Ethiopians were occasional informants for European interlocutors, who in turn limited themselves to presenting mediated fragments of collected testimony. The Psalter, in contrast, required an intensive and sustained collaboration between a European, who could navigate the institutional aspects of the printing process, and an Ethiopian, who could prepare a reliable Ge'ez text and review the newly created type for the Ethiopian script, or fidäl. In short, it required co-authorship.

At the same time, the Psalter inaugurated an enduring shift toward text and language in Ethiopianist research. While it was a devotional text for the Santo Stefano community,[130] it also contained prefatory language materials intended for European readers. These include Latin introductions to the Ge'ez language and fidäl script, suggesting a pedagogic function that paralleled Tomas's role as Potken's language tutor. Yet the student soon effaced the teacher. After printing the Psalter in Rome, Potken returned to Germany, where he issued a 1518 synoptic edition of the Psalter in Latin, Ge'ez, Greek, and Hebrew, omitting any reference to his Ethiopian collaborator and modifying the fidäl script to account for sixth-order vocalization.[131] This edition in turn became a standard reference for Ge'ez language study in sixteenth-century Europe.[132] It notably underpins Postel's 1538 *Linguarum duodecim characteribus differentium alphabetum*, a polyglot language manual that presents the fidäl and Ge'ez language materials from the 1513 Tomas-Potken Psalter in a comparative linguistic framework, highlights the similarities between Ge'ez and Hebrew, and offers Latin translations of the Prayer of Simeon, Psalm 42, and Psalm

---

[129] Potken and Tomas Wäldä Samu'él, *Psalterium*, unpaginated leaf: "ላዝንቱ ዳዊት ተሀትመ በገረ ሮማ ዮሐንስ ጶትቁን አሌማንያዊ ጸሬጽሲቶስ ቤተ ክርስቲአኡ ቅዱስ ጊዮርጊስ በገረ ኮሎንያ በአሌማንያ ወምስሌሁ ሁተመ አነ ቶማስ ወልዱ ለሳሙኤል ገዳማዊ ነገዱ ኢየሩሳሌም አመ ዐ ለወርኅ ሐምሌ ዐመት ለኢየሱስ ክርስቶስ አምላክነ ወልደ እግዚአብሔር ወማርያም ድንግል ፲፻፭፻፲፫ አሜን።" On this statement as Tomas's "final act of self-affirmation," see Kelly, *Translating Faith*, 129.
[130] BAV, Vat. Et. 66, 2v. [131] Potken, *Psalterium in Quatuor Linguis*.
[132] Contini, "Linguistica semitica," 49.

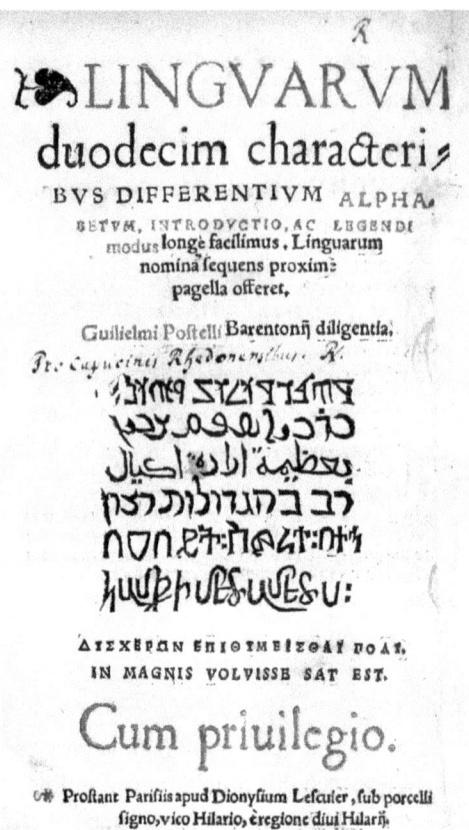

Figure 7 Title Page, Guillaume Postel, *Linguarum duodecim characteribus differentium alphabetum* (Paris: Dionysium Lescuier, 1538)

116 (Figure 7).[133] Postel's work is considered one of the first European contributions to comparative Semitic linguistics.[134]

Political developments complemented these shifts in the structure of knowledge. After the Portuguese embassy reached Lebnä Dengel in 1520, a flood of publications celebrated this event as the epochal discovery of Prester John. These included Manuel I's letter to Pope Leo X;[135] the reports of Andrea Corsali (1487-nd.), a papal representative attached to the Portuguese delegation;[136] and

---

[133] Postel, *Linguarum duodecim*, unpaginated discussion of "De Indica lingua." Postel's use of the 1513 edition is indicated by the fact that his Ge'ez text does not reproduce an error in the 1518 edition of Psalm 42:2: "እስመ እንተ አምላኪየ ወኃይያ [ወኃይልየ] ለምንት ተኃድገኒ"

[134] Secret, "Études arabes"; Contini, "Linguistica semitica." [135] Manuel, *Presbytero Ioanne*.

[136] Corsali, *Iuliano de Medici*; Corsali, *Laurentio de Medici*.

the correspondence of two agents of the Estado da Índia who accompanied the delegation to present-day Eritrea.[137] When the embassy returned to Lisbon in 1527, it brought a putative letter of papal submission from Lebnä Dengel, an apparent affirmation of the universal church and the era's fervid Prestermania.[138] Yet this understanding was soon shattered by *liqä kahenat* Şägga Zä'ab (ca. 1465/75–ca.1539/45), an Ethiopian ecclesiastic and ambassador who reached Lisbon with the returning Portuguese delegation. He befriended the court intellectual Damião de Góis (1502–74), who published a Latin apologia for Ethiopian Christianity that included Şägga Zä'ab's confession of faith as well as an account of the Solomonid dynasty and its link to the Biblical Solomon and Sheba.[139] This 1540 defence of Ethiopian Orthodoxy was censored by the Inquisitor General,[140] but Şägga Zä'ab's revelations suggested that the real Lebnä Dengel did not resemble the imagined Prester John. Likewise, news of the Ottoman–Adal invasion also undermined the myth of a mighty Christian potentate who could advance the global anti-Islamic crusade.

These developments fueled an explosion of new scholarship. By the late 1530s, the European field of Ethiopia-focused research was no longer the obscure purview of minor figures; instead, it had become a prominent arena of historico-religious debate attuned to the dynamics of imperial diplomacy. If this shift was broadly exemplified by Postel's incorporation of Ethiopian languages and texts within his heretical universalist framework, it was more specifically attested by the memoir of Portuguese chaplain Francisco Álvares (1465–1536/41), who penned the first European eyewitness and proto-ethnographic description of the Horn. It was published in Lisbon in 1540,[141] after substantial cuts by the censor.[142] Unlike the societies of Asia and the Americas, highland Ethiopia had initially seemed to possess a superficial resemblance to European Christendom, with an integrated church and state, a highly developed monastic culture and scribal tradition, and an exotic but lineally adjacent Christian faith. Increased contact instead exposed Europeans to a messier reality, the details of which became an arena of charged scholarly disputation.

Paolo Giovio, Ludovico Beccadelli, and Marcello Cervini

This was the heated climate that surrounded Täsfa Şeyon in Rome. His intervention in the 1536 Bermudes affair began a fourteen-year period of intense intellectual activity, in which he worked with leading figures in the burgeoning field of Ethiopia-focused research. Among the first of these was historian Paolo

---

[137] Sequeria and Gomes Teixeira, *Abyssinia*. [138] Marcocci, "Umanisti italiani," 317–18.
[139] Góis, *Fides, religio, moresque Aethiopum*. [140] Marcocci, "Umanisti italiani," 362–63.
[141] Álvares, *Ho Preste Ioam*. [142] Aubin, "Prêtre Jean," 36–37.

Figure 8 Cristofano di Papi dell'Altissimo, *Paolo Giovio*, ca. 1560, Galleria degli Uffizi, Firenze

Giovio (1483–1552) (Figure 8). Hailing from Como, Giovio began his career as the physician of Cardinal Giulio de' Medici (1478–1534), the future Pope Clement VII. This role brought him to Rome, where he embraced the era's fascination with the discovered wider world, including Ethiopia. His curial position made him privy to Corsali's 1516 and 1518 dispatches on the Portuguese delegation to Ethiopia, and he surely read the dramatic publications on the discovery of Prester John. He first mentioned Ethiopia in an unpublished 1527 cultural history of Italy, wherein he describes "Armenians and Ethiopians living in the area of the Vatican occupied by pottery workshops," referring to the environs of Santo Stefano.[143] Six years later, in 1533, he contributed to a pamphlet celebrating Lebnä Dengel's presumed papal submission.[144]

A more substantial discussion followed in his *Historiarum sui temporis* (1550).[145] This innovative work was an early attempt at unifying European and extra-European history within a global narrative, exemplifying a wider sixteenth-century shift from universal to world historiography.[146] At a time when most local historians wrote dynastic histories based on archival sources and official chronicles, and when universal historians conceptualized world history from the perspective of an outward-looking home society, Giovio

---

[143] Giovio, *Dialogo,* 418–19; Bandini, "Notizie," 502.
[144] Keymolen, *Legatio David*; Keymolen, *Ambasciaria di David.*   [145] Giovio, *Historiarum.*
[146] Marcocci, *Globe on Paper*; Subrahmanyam, "World Historians."

instead exploited Rome's location as a cosmopolitan and imperial crossroads to aggregate extant knowledge with the testimony of foreign visitors and the fruit of the expanding Vatican intelligence network.

This dynamic underpins the Ethiopian section of the *Historiarum*. After a troglodyte-filled "Description of Africa," Giovio soberly turned to "the empires of the great Prester John."[147] Although he exaggerated the size and built environment of the Christian kingdom, claiming it reached the Cape of Good Hope and comprised "many palaces and very magnificent temples," he also reported that Prester John resided in "pavilions," clearly referencing the itinerant imperial *kätäma*. He precisely situated the latter in Shäwa, the ancestral home and power base of Lebnä Dengel, and added that the church "patriarch" lived in its royal capital Bärara, south of present-day Addis Ababa.[148] This was likely a reference to the seat of metropolitan *abunä* Gabr'él.[149] This mixture of fantasy and fact pervades the text. For example, Giovio claimed "Pretegian" [Prester John] was a corruption of "Beldugian," an "ancient nickname usurped from past kings," and itself a possible corruption of the Amharic *bädel jan*, meaning "victorious majesty." Similarly, he alleged that Gojjam was inhabited by "big dragons with wings, who walk the ground with webbed feet like geese," but then offered a reasonable account of recent Solomonid history, noting the reigns of Gälawdéwos and Lebnä Dengel (Figure 9) as well as their immediate predecessors Emperor Na'od (1494–1508) and Queen Eléni (1431–1522), and describing events such as the Adal invasion and the deaths of Lebnä Dengel and 'Aḥmad Grañ.[150]

While Giovio's fantastic claims elaborated the Prester John mythology, their underlying Judeo-Christian eschatology, and the received classical understanding of Africa, his surer descriptions derived from the testimony of informed observers. One was Álvares; another was Täsfa Ṣeyon. In a portrait that suggests some acquaintance, Giovio introduced the latter as

> a man of honorable and illustrious ingenuity, [who] with great humanity and faith told me notable things about the Abyssinians. Knowing many languages, and having become a friar in Rome, he learned our language very well, and taught the Abyssinian language to some of our curious men. ... Since the oriental Christian pilgrims in Rome, and in particular the Abyssinians, have their own church and house behind the dome of Saint Peter's, where they celebrate [mass] according to their custom, [they] are supported at the pope's expense and with great humanity by the prelates of the [papal] court.[151]

---

[147] Giovio, *Historie*, 524v, 526v.   [148] Giovio, *Historie*, 531r; Deresse Ayenachew, "Kätäma."
[149] Kur, ed., *Marha Krestos*, Vol. 1, 36.   [150] Giovio, *Historie*, 528v–34.
[151] Giovio, *Historie* 528rv.

Figure 9 Portrait of Lebnä Dengel in Paolo Giovio's museum, Cristofano di Papi dell'Altissimo, *L'Imperatore Atana de Dinghel*, ca. 1560, Galleria degli Uffizi, Firenze

The *mämher*'s contributions to the *Historiarum* are sometimes readily discerned. Álvares might have been able to describe life in the Solomonid court, but only Täsfa Ṣeyon could have convinced Giovio that Shäwa was "deemed very noble and better than all the others for its fertility, good regions[,] and its inhabitants' ingenuity."[152] In a suggestion of an autochthonous ethnic ontology, Giovio also reported that Shäwans "preceded all Abyssinians in astuteness, ingenuity, sobriety, customs[,] and good-living," and "rule no different than Venetian gentlemen."[153]

Giovio's historiographic fusion suggests the durability of canonical knowledge in an era of intellectual change. The shocking new discoveries about the societies of the Americas and Asia strained but did not immediately overturn Europeans' inherited models of the wider world, and the intellectual work of reconciling new reports and local sources with canonical texts and inherited forms of learning proved slow and inconsistent.[154] Ancient learning and medieval fantasies were resilient, and often persisted alongside the latest scholarship – even within the genre of observational travel writing. Despite

---

[152] Giovio, *Historie*, 526v.
[153] Giovio, *Historie*, 527r. This did not exhaust his Ethiophilia: see also the Lebnä Dengel portrait (Figure 10) and eulogy in Giovio, *Elogia*, 310–11.
[154] Grafton, *New Worlds*, 93; Tinguely, *Écriture du Levant*.

LIBER VI.
Dauid Maximus Abyſſino-
rum Aethiopum Rex.

ETHIOPES cucullati Sacerdotes qui poſt maximum Vaticani templum ſedem & delubrum habent, communi conſenſu eam ſui Regis effigiem veriſsimam affirmant, quam Petrus Aluares Legatus cum cruce aurea ad Clementem Pontificem detulit. Is poſtea nobis ex commentario Abyſsinorum regiones & mores explicauit,quæ omnia à nobis in Hiſtorijs ſuo loco ita diffuſe enarrata ſunt, vt nihil quod ad digniſsimarum rerum noticiam pertinere poſsit deſiderari queat;qua de re, in exprimendo Dauide aſtrictiore vtemur Elogio,ne his faſtidio ſim, qui hiſtorias noſtras perlegerint. Hoc autem de eo Rege totius cogniti orbis longe maximo, dici poteſt, quod non modò Chriſtianæ religionis dogmata & cerimonias profitcri, ſed his prope iuris ciuilis legibus, & vti nos diſciplinæ militaris inſtitutis, tot ſua

Gg 4

Figure 10 Portrait of Lebnä Dengel in Paolo Giovio, *Pavli Iovii Novocomensis episcopi nvcerini, Elogia virorum bellica virtute illustrium* (Basel: Petri Pernae typographi, 1575) (photo by the author)

its cutting-edge elements, Giovio's history of Ethiopia still reflected traditional authorities. Moreover, unlike his contemporaries Postel and Potken, Giovio operated outside the field of *philologia sacra* and was largely uninterested in its soteriological approach to Eastern Christianity and Muslim–Christian relations. Instead, he wrote history to distract the European reader from "so many bloody wars and sad events [with] a digression of a more pleasant subject."[155] He had a penchant for the exotic, but he was not an orientalist.

In this, his motivation differed from his contemporary Ludovico Beccadelli (1501–72). A curial personality from Bologna, Beccadelli was the secretary of Cardinal Gasparo Contarini (1483–1542). The latter was a leading member of the *spirituali*, a circle of lay and ordained figures committed to humanism, ecumenism, and church reform, and whose broad intellectual interests and personal quest for salvation have led to their characterization as a "religious republic of letters."[156] In opposition to their conservative rivals the *zelanti*, who rejected accommodation and championed strict orthodoxy, the *spirituali* critiqued the debased state of the church, sought accommodation with the Protestants, and hoped for ecumenical reunification with the Eastern Churches.

Ethiopia was central to this last undertaking. The connection was first intimated by *spirituali* forefather Erasmus of Rotterdam (1466–1536), who in his *Ecclesiastae* (1535) sympathetically reported that the "King of Ethiopia" had once informed the pontiff of his people's long neglect.[157] Contarini in turn embraced the project of Eastern Christian reunification, and specifically identified the Council of Florence as a model for Protestant reconciliation.[158] In 1540, his belief in Ethiopia's ecumenical potential led him to summon another Ethiopian ecclesiastic named *abba* Yoḥannes of Cyprus (1509–65), also known as Giovanni Battista Abissino, from Venice to Rome, where the latter eventually became a colleague of Täsfa Seyon and the *rayes* of Santo Stefano.[159]

Around this same time, Beccadelli acquired a disorganized Italian manuscript version of Álvares's then-unpublished *Ho Preste Ioam das Indias: verdadera informaçam das terras do Preste Ioam* (1540). In all likelihood, it was a translation the Portuguese left unfinished upon his death in Rome in the mid-1530s.[160] When discovered by Beccadelli, it was a unique work based on the authority of eyewitness reportage. He spent twenty years revising it. As he explained:

> [I] ordered, divided, and made it as much clear as I could, only by adding a few things in certain places, where our Ethiopians in Rome disagree with

---

[155] Giovio, *Historie*, 524r.   [156] Furey, *Republic of Letters*, 13.
[157] Erasmus, *Ecclesiastae*, 105.   [158] Gleason, *Contarini*, 151.
[159] Salvadore, "African Cosmopolitanism," 72.
[160] Álvares, *Historia*, 12–14; Natta, "Beccadelli," 297–308.

what is written [in the manuscript text]. Because you must know that to be faithful to the truth and my satisfaction, I confirmed it with our good Ethiopian, brother Pietro [Täsfa Ṣeyon], and others of his [community].[161]

These consultations produced forty-two additions to the original text.[162] While Beccadelli's version improved the transliteration of Ethiopian terms and added new details about the fate of the Portuguese delegation, most of his changes addressed controversial aspects of Ethiopian Orthodox doctrine and practice. In this, Beccadelli offered a *spirituali* counter to Vatican critics of Ethiopian Christianity,[163] produced in the aftermath of Ṣägga Zä'ab and Góis's censored apologia, and mobilizing the intellectual authority of Beccadelli's diasporic informants. For example, he explains that the Ethiopian ritual of annual baptism at Ṭemqät was not sacramental, but was instead meant "to commemorate the baptism of Christ."[164] As for the practices of scarification and tattooing, Beccadelli explained that the Ethiopians at Santo Stefano said these were "done to improve the eyesight, for different traditions, and for beauty," while "brother Pietro [Täsfa Ṣeyon] said that they are done ... to distinguish themselves from other tribes, as much of Ethiopia regards as enemies those [descendants of the] ancient Jews who came to Ethiopia with the son of Solomon [Menilek]."[165] These comments addressed persistent European confusion about forehead branding as a form of baptism by fire.[166]

Despite the significance of these insights for the European understanding of Ethiopian Christianity, Beccadelli's project never appeared in print.[167] As a contribution to the Ethiopianist library, its value was diminished by Álvares's *Ho Preste Ioam das Indias*, which appeared alongside Leo Africanus's history in the first volume of the best-selling *Delle navigationi et viaggi* (1550), edited by Giovanni Battista Ramusio (1485–1557).[168] But Beccadelli's ecumenical editing was also out-of-step with the strident Tridentine mood, as suggested by the fact that the Portuguese edition of Álvares's manuscript was only published in a mutilated form, while Ṣägga Zä'ab's confession was censored outright. Perhaps Beccadelli did not publish in hope of evading the newly established Roman Inquisition. By the 1550s, its Venetian counterpart had arrested Postel and dispatched him to the cells of the Castel Sant'Angelo, just a short walk from Santo Stefano at the Tiber.[169]

---

[161] BAV, Ott. Lat. 2789, ir.   [162] BAV, Ott. Lat. 2789, 113r–116v.
[163] Already suggested in Natta, "Beccadelli," 289–94.   [164] BAV, Ott. Lat. 2789, 115v.
[165] BAV, Ott. Lat. 2789, 113r.   [166] Hamilton, *Copts and the West*, 111–18.
[167] Natta, "Beccadelli," 297–308.   [168] Ramusio, *Navigationi*.   [169] Kuntz, *Postel*, 17.

Figure 11 Jacopino Del Conte (attributed), *Cardinal Marcello Cervini degli Spannocchi*, Galleria Borghese, Rome (photo by Mauro Coen)

If the Roman elite increasingly disdained the Solomonid dynasty and Ethiopian Christianity, their interest in Ethiopia remained undiminished. Instead, Tridentine Catholic intellectual politics produced a new impetus for understanding Ethiopia and Eastern Christianity, transforming the antecedent exoticist and ecumenical Prestermania. The leading patron of this new orientation was Marcello Cervini (1501–55), the future Pope Marcellus II (Figure 11), who began his ecclesiastic ascent after 1534 when his patron Alessandro Farnese assumed the papacy. This development won Cervini several key curial positions, culminating in his elevation to the cardinalate in 1539, after which he led the Council of Trent (1545–63) and the Vatican negotiations with the Protestants. In 1546 he joined the Roman Inquisition, and in 1548 he was appointed head of the Biblioteca Vaticana, where he dedicated himself to establishing its collection of oriental manuscripts.[170] In 1555, he ascended to the papacy for twenty-two days.

Cervini's interest in Ethiopia exemplifies his intellectual complexity. He was at once an unwavering humanist, a quasi-orientalist, a sponsor of the printed word, and an avatar of militant Tridentine Catholicism. This contradiction has generated controversy with respect to his position in the *spirituali-zelanti*

---

[170] Sachet, *Publishing for the Popes*, 173.

struggle.[171] Although he developed a profound interest in classical, patristic, and Eastern Christian texts,[172] and even dabbled with Chinese,[173] his earliest Vatican-sponsored publications were staunch defences of papal authority, such as the letters of Nicholas I (1542) and Innocent III (1543), and Henry VIII's defence of the sacraments (1543).[174] Yet by the mid-1540s, he also began to pursue the acquisition, study, and publication of Greek, Syriac, and Ge'ez texts that would aid his position at Trent.

In service of this undertaking, Cervini rallied orientalists like Postel as well as intermediary figures in the Eastern Christian diaspora. He supported the Syriac Orthodox deacon Petrus of Damascus's Roman sojourn, and recommended him as an Arabic translator to the German scholar Johann Widmannstetter (1506–57).[175] Cervini also collaborated with Petrus's coreligionist Moses of Mārdīn, and sponsored the latter's 1555 print edition of the Syriac New Testament, produced with the aid of Postel.[176] Upon assuming the papacy as Marcellus II, he planned to continue harnessing the imprimatur of Eastern Christian texts, including the publication of patristic works in line with Catholic dogma, including editions of unpublished works by John Chrysostom, widely influential in the Orthodox world.[177] These pursuits unfolded alongside the broader question of Catholic communion with Greek, Armenian, Coptic, and Syriac Orthodox Christians and the perceived utility of these relationships as models of interdenominational fraternity.

Cervini also instrumentalized the Ethiopianist library, using Täsfa Ṣeyon to advance his ecclesiastic agenda. In 1546, Guglielmo Sirleto (1514–85), custodian of the Biblioteca Apostolica Vaticana, dispatched a letter to Cervini in Trent. He explained that the *mämher* of Rome had just acquired a Ge'ez manuscript containing the Nicene canons, which included "eighty four [canons] beyond the twenty we already had," one of which "speaks of the primacy of the Roman Church above any other."[178] Sirleto tasked Täsfa Ṣeyon with translating this manuscript into Latin. Although we lack Cervini's reply, Sirleto was clearly acting on his superior's input. This point is suggested by a letter that same year from Cervini to Bernardino Maffei (1514–53), the secretary of Paul III:

> I would like you to have the Indian [Ethiopian] and Maronite masses translated, to see if those provinces, converted by different apostles, have the same substance we have in terms of sacrifice, the intercession of saints[,]

---

[171] Quaranta, *Cervini*, 25–126. [172] Paschini, "Cardinale editore."
[173] Sachet, *Publishing for the Popes*, 181. [174] Paschini, "Cardinale editore," 392.
[175] Cardinali, "Cervini," 79–83.
[176] Wilkinson, *Orientalism*, 64–75, 131–33; Cardinali, *Cardinale maraviglioso*, 200–205.
[177] Sachet, *Publishing for the Popes*, 194; Kennerley, *John Chrysostom*.
[178] Guglielmo Sirleto to Marcello Cervini, July 9, 1547, Rome, BAV, Vat. Lat. 6177, 313r.

and the prayers for the dead. If I remember correctly brother Peter [Täsfa Ṣeyon] ... told me they [Ethiopians] have in the mass all these things. When we will deal of these things, it will be better to be informed.[179]

The reference is a tantalizing clue. Not only was Täsfa Ṣeyon in dialogue with the powerbroker orientalist-cardinal, but the latter instructed his collaborators to enlist the Ethiopian's doctrinal and linguistic expertise in the ongoing effort to defend papal supremacy through the study of Eastern Christian texts. In a striking coincidence, Täsfa Ṣeyon conferred that very same year with the ex-Jesuit and emerging arch-heretic Postel, who was then using esoteric eastern texts to attack papal supremacy as "the greatest sin in the world."[180] The *mämher* was thus enlisted by both sides of the leading intellectual battle of the church. In the process, he was thrust into the center of the emerging world of Vatican-coordinated orientalist scholarship, as epitomized by his collaboration with Cervini, its leading architect. The result was three ground-breaking printed books.

Täsfa Ṣeyon and the Ge'ez Gospels

Täsfa Ṣeyon's magnum opus was the *Testamentum Novum* (1548), a monumental Latin-Ge'ez work of nearly 500 pages, featuring fidäl type, red and black ink, and woodcut illustrations (Figure 12). It is the *editio princeps* of the Ge'ez Gospels. Initially issued as an incomplete edition in 1548, its second and final edition appeared in 1549 with the appended Pauline Epistles, absent from the first edition because of a delay in procuring the source manuscript. The contents of the full edition include Latin and Ge'ez introductions and dedications; a Latin introduction to fidäl that drew upon and corrected the corresponding section of the 1513 Psalter; the Ge'ez Eusebian canon tables, which identify corresponding passages in the four Gospels; the Ge'ez Gospels, Book of Revelation, and Acts of the Apostles; the Ethiopian Mass; the Pauline Epistles; and concluding dedications, again in Latin and Ge'ez. The Latin and Ge'ez introductions and conclusions vary substantially. The individual Gospels, Book of Revelation, and Acts are followed by Ge'ez statements by Täsfa Ṣeyon, which generally indicate the date of completion, list the individuals involved, and offer thanks to a range of benefactors and collaborators. Some of these statements resemble colophons; others are longer commentaries.[181]

---

[179] Marcello Cervini to Bernardino Maffei, March 14, 1546, Trent, ASF, Carte Cerviniane 19, 28r.
[180] Kuntz, *Postel*, 63.
[181] Similar statements appear in other Ge'ez manuscripts from the Santo Stefano library, in keeping with the norms of Ethiopian scribal culture: BAV, Vat. Et. 5, 69v; BAV, Vat. Et. 25, 248v.

TESTAMENTVM
NOVVM CVM EPISTOLA PAVLI AD

Hebreos tantum, cum concordantijs Euangeliſtarum Euſebij & numeratione omnium verborum eorundem. Miſſale cum benedictione incenſi ceræ et c. Alphaꝛ betum in lingua ግእዝ:gheez, ideſt libera quia a nulla alia originem duxit, & vulgo dicitur Chaldea, Quæ omnia Fr̃ Petrus Ethyops auxilio piorum ſedente Paulo.III.Pont. Max. & Claudio illius regni Imꝑ peratore imprimi curauit.

ANNO SALVTIS M. D. XLVIII.

Figure 12 Title page dedicated to Pope Paul III, Petrus Ethyops [Täsfa Ṣeyon], *Testamentum Novum cum Epistola Pauli ad Hebreos* [...] (Rome: Valerius Doricus, 1548), BAV, Membr.IV.14 (Photo by author)

The *Testamentum Novum* consumed Täsfa Ṣeyon's final years in Rome. It emerged from an extended collaboration with Tänśe'a Wäld and Zäśellasé, both from the Ethiopian community in Rome, as well as Pietro Paolo Gualtieri, the *mäggabi* of Santo Stefano, and Mariano Vittori (1503/11–1572), a *spirituale* subordinate of cardinal Reginald Pole (1500–58).[182] Their work was challenging, beginning with the question of source texts. Ge'ez manuscripts typically reached Rome via Ethiopian pilgrims, and by the mid-sixteenth century, Santo Stefano boasted a sizeable library of codices.[183] Täsfa Ṣeyon himself gave the community a manuscript containing the Ge'ez Gospels.[184] Manuscripts also arrived in the hands of Europeans returning from Ethiopia and the Holy Land, as in the case of Potken and Tomas Wäldä Samu'él's Psalter.[185] For the *Testamentum Novum*, Täsfa Ṣeyon drew upon the Santo Stefano library for the Ge'ez Gospels, Revelation, Catholic and Hebrew Epistles, Acts, and Mass,[186] but was obliged to procure a source manuscript with the Pauline Epistles from Cyprus, drawing upon his compatriot Yoḥannes of Cyprus and the latter's ecclesiastic and diasporic network.[187]

A second challenge concerned the production of the printed Ge'ez text. This was among the most arduous aspects of the work. As the *mämher* lamented: "You should know that we worked day and night, with hardship and pain, I, Täsfa Ṣeyon, and Tänśe'a Wäld with Zäśellasé; and we printed and [even] contributed to the publication with a *wäqét* of gold."[188] Apart from the labor and expense of casting fidäl moveable type, the latter presented unique difficulties for the workshop compositors, who found themselves setting type they could not read. The only local printers with fidäl experience were the Silber brothers, who had produced the 1513 Psalter, but they left the industry after the 1527 Sack of Rome, when the city's printing industry lost much of its base of technical expertise.[189] Given this situation, Täsfa Ṣeyon turned to the Dorico brothers, leading Roman printers who were unfamiliar with fidäl. It is easy to imagine the Ethiopians painstakingly reviewing the Ge'ez type in the printers' workshop. To the Italian compositors, the text surely resembled hieroglyphs. Täsfa Ṣeyon likened their shared linguistic and technical endeavor to "the blind helping each other."[190]

While working on the *Testamentum Novum*, Täsfa Ṣeyon also completed two shorter Latin works, *Missa qua Ethiopes* (1549) and *Modus baptizandi* (1549). These were, respectively, a translation of the Ethiopian mass published in the *Testamentum Novum*, based on Vat. Et. 16,[191] and a translation of the Ethiopian baptismal rite, based on Vat. Et. 4.[192] These projects had occupied Täsfa Ṣeyon since at least 1547, when they emerged in the Cervini-Sirleto

---

[182] *TN*, 226r; Sassetti, *Vittori*, 30–31.   [183] BAV, Vat. Et. 66, 2v.   [184] BAV, Vat. Et. 16, 61v.
[185] BAV, Vat. Et. 20; Lefevre, "De Brocchi," 69–70.   [186] Kelly, *Translating Faith*, 242–43.
[187] Yoḥannes of Cyprus to Täsfa Ṣeyon, December 15, 1548, Venice, BI, MS D, V, 13, 253r. See Online Appendix Item 3.
[188] *TN*, unpaginated Ge'ez preface.   [189] Barberi, "Libri e stampatori," 222.
[190] *TN*, unpaginated Ge'ez preface.
[191] Grébaut and Tisserant, *Codices aethiopici*, Vol. 1, 61–65.   [192] Grébaut, "Baptême," 2.

correspondence.[193] In translating the Ge'ez mass and baptism rituals, Täsfa Ṣeyon again collaborated with two Europeans: Gualtieri, who is identified as the co-translator of the Ethiopian mass, and who was in the judgment of Vittori the only other European competent in Ge'ez;[194] and Bernardino Sander, a copyist from Cremona and friend of Täsfa Ṣeyon[195] who helped translate the baptism, and who in the Ethiopian's assessment had some knowledge of Ge'ez.[196] Sirleto supervised both editions, even as Cervini requested a second translation of the Ge'ez mass ritual from Yoḥannes of Cyprus.[197] To print the editions, the *mämher* selected Antonio Blado (1515–67), the official printer of the Apostolic Chamber and recipient of past Cervini commissions,[198] widely recognized in Rome as the publisher of Ignatius of Loyola's *Exercitia spiritualia* (1548) and Niccolò Machiavelli's *Discorsi* (1531). In 1549, the Blado workshop issued the *Missa* and *Modus baptizandi* in a single volume, accompanied by Täsfa Ṣeyon's Latin translation of the 1542 letter from Gälawdéwos. Unlike the *Testamentum Novum*, which features hundreds of pages of fidäl text, the *Missa* and *Modus baptizandi* were short and nearly entirely in Latin. They were for this reason readily reprintable, as a 1550 Louvain edition suggests.

What inspired this Ethiopian embrace of the printed word? The complexity of Täsfa Ṣeyon's purpose is suggested by the diversity of his imagined readers. The problem is starkly illustrated in the final pages of the *Testamentum Novum*. Täsfa Ṣeyon begins its Ge'ez conclusion with an eminently Ethiopian Orthodox – and thus *täwaḥedo* or Miaphysite – Christology affirming "three persons and one substance and two births."[199] This statement invokes the distinctive "two births" doctrine, which holds that Jesus was born first to God in heaven without a mother, and second to the Virgin Mary on earth without a father, in a single and unified nature.[200] Täsfa Ṣeyon follows this with a second Latin conclusion wherein he affirms "three persons of one substance and twofold nativity."[201] Intriguingly, his use of the Latin *nativitas*, meaning birth but also implying a natural or innate quality, would allow a Catholic reader to potentially understand this second Christological statement as properly Chalcedonian, even as an Ethiopian reader would understand it as Miaphysite, in that the concept of "two births" – but not dual nature – was dogmatic for the

---

[193] BAV, Vat. Lat. 6177, 310–350; Vat. Lat. 6178, 117–122.
[194] Victorius, *Chaldeae*, unpaginated leaf; *Modus baptizandi*.
[195] Bernardinello, *Autografi*, 27; *TN*, unpaginated Ge'ez frontispiece. [196] *Modus baptizandi*.
[197] Sachet, *Publishing for the Popes*, 176–77; Kelly, *Translating Faith*, 248–49.
[198] Paschini, "Cardinale editore."
[199] *TN*, 225r: "በሥሉስቱ ገጽ ወበአሐዱ ኅለዌ ወበተወልደ ምንትው አአምን"
[200] Proverbs 8:22–24; Luke 1:30–31.
[201] *TN*, 226r: "In tribus personis una substantia et duplici nativitate credo."

Ethiopian church.[202] The two confessions of faith were thus exquisitely attuned to the heated doctrinal politics of Ethiopia and Europe, and in this respect, they paralleled similarly accommodating aspects of Täsfa Ṣeyon's Latin missal text.[203] If the differences reflected his awareness of the censors and the limits of their language competencies, they also reveal the complexity of the *mämher*'s envisioned audiences.

The most immediate of these was the community of Ethiopian pilgrims at Santo Stefano, for whom the *Testamentum Novum* was a revolutionary devotional text. With respect to its material form, it was uniquely suited to the worldly needs of a transient diasporic reader: its legible fidäl and small physical size[204] made it uniquely portable, such that it could be easily carried by hand or pocket.[205] This readership is also suggested by its Ge'ez introduction, wherein Täsfa Ṣeyon beseeched "his brothers"[206] to forgive his editorial failings, and additionally its Ge'ez conclusion, wherein he counted himself among the "uprooted Ethiopian[s]" in foreign lands.[207] This rhetoric of diasporic fellowship is absent from the Latin introduction and conclusion, which are instead addressed to a "pious and Christian reader."[208] In a further gesture to his diasporic kin, Täsfa Ṣeyon adhered to *liqawent* norms of authorship and reading, adapting manuscript practice to the printed page. His introductory supplication replicated the scribal convention of asking readers and/or God to forgive his errors, gesturing toward the collective scholarly endeavor of pious inquiry and rigorous transmission of sacred texts, and he paired the Gospels with the Eusebian canon tables, following the Ethiopian paratextual convention. The *Testamentum Novum*'s warm reception by the pilgrims is suggested by the fact that the Santo Stefano library used its copy to preserve the community rule, handwritten in both Ge'ez and Latin in its final pages.[209]

But Täsfa Ṣeyon also envisioned readers in Ethiopia. Broadly, this orientation is suggested by the dedications to Gälawdéwos in the *Testamentum Novum*, which acknowledge the emperor's popular European identification with Prester John.[210] But more specifically, his Ge'ez commentaries throughout outline a vision of the text as an instrument of salvific Ethiopian renewal, as he repeatedly termed it.[211] The context for this intervention rested upon his equation of contemporary Ethiopia and ancient Israel. After the Acts of the

---

[202] Mebratu Kiros Gebru, *Miaphysite Christology*, 36–41.
[203] For a thorough discussion of this aspect of the *Missa*, see Kelly, *Translating Faith*, 251–54.
[204] It measures approximately 18 by 22 cm. [205] Samuel Asghedom, "Santo Stefano," 399.
[206] "ወንአሙ-ዮ" [207] *TN*, 225r: "ኢትዮጲያዊ ፈሲሲ [ኢትዮጵያዊ ፈሲሲ]"
[208] *TN*, unpaginated Latin incipit: "Christiano et pio lectori"
[209] BAV, R.I.IV 2218, 227r–229v. [210] *TN*, 176r, 225r, 226v. [211] *TN*, 100r: "ሐደሰ"

Apostles, which concludes with Paul's proclamation of Christianity in Rome, Täsfa Ṣeyon writes:

> We have seen the devastation of our country, the destruction of our books and disappearance [sic] of the Word of God from our country[,] as perished during the Babylonian exile [of Israel]. But God renewed [Israel] by the hand of Ezra, the prophet. Likewise, we did [this book] and published [it] in commemoration [of the restoration of Ethiopia], and we printed [it] with much suffering, much hardship, and much cost; we do it tenaciously [since] we received it [i.e., the Gospels] from our forefathers ... Likewise/in this, [we] improve that which we inherited from our forefathers when all [of us] are diligent for our people.[212]

In this understanding, the *Testamentum Novum* contributed to the tradition of transmitting sacred texts, reaching from the exiled Ezra through the "forefathers" of the church to Täsfa Ṣeyon and his sixteenth-century collaborators, whose print edition was a historic and epochal act of stewardship inspired by the ancient scribe-priest. A complimentary vision underpins Täsfa Ṣeyon's commentary after the Gospel of John, wherein he likens 'Aḥmad Grañ and the Muslims of Adal to the "pagans" of Babylon.[213]

This potent historical imaginary is further developed in his commentary after the Book of Revelation. He there narrates the ancient Israelites' return from the Babylonian exile, culminating in the rebuilding of the Temple and the reedition of scripture and transmission of religious law by Ezra. Together, these events constituted the restoration of Israel. After this historical survey, Täsfa Ṣeyon turns to his ancestral home. He emotively laments:

> My mother, holy Ethiopia, you delivered me. I am alive by the mouth [i.e., words] of your rule from our father. The pilgrims [here in Rome] inform about you [mother Ethiopia], with your *neguś* Gäläwdéwos [Gälawdéwos], the overlord; he [re]built Däbrä Libanos by the hand of Enbaqom, with many fathers, with all the chosen. May your God bring you back all your dispersed [and] destroyed people. So be it. Amen.[214]

Read closely and in tandem with the Acts and John commentaries, this passage suggests the role of the *Testamentum Novum* in Ethiopia's future, in keeping with the temporal orientation of Revelation. Again comparing ancient Israel to sixteenth-century Ethiopia, Täsfa Ṣeyon intertwines these two chosen nations and their struggle against "pagan" adversaries: the Ethiopians were presently "dispersed" in suffering and exile, like their ancient forbears, but their return to the promised land was now imminent, as suggested by the reconstruction of

---

[212] *TN*, 157v. [213] *TN*, 100v: "አረሚ". See Online Appendix Item 4. [214] *TN*, 113r.

Däbrä Libanos, here the Ethiopian Temple.[215] This renewal would encompass the restoration of the Solomonids and return of the exiled Ethiopians of Rome and Jerusalem. This aspect is suggested by his implicit self-analogy to the unreturned Ezra, as an ecclesiastic counterpart to Gälawdéwos and the would-be restorer of destroyed texts to "Mother Ethiopia."[216] It is more broadly signaled by his self-description as *fälasi*, or "uprooted," using the same verb that is used to describe the Israelite exile in the Ge'ez Bible.[217] In a further indication of this imagination, he elsewhere adopted the moniker *malḥazo*, a Ge'ez neologism that would appear to mean "the exiled/removed one," as a personal identifier of his own uprootedness.[218] These expressions elaborated an Ethiopian vernacular of diasporic identity, adapting the scriptural language of Israelite exile to the exigencies of early modern displacement.

If the *Testamentum Novum* was intended to save Ethiopian readers, the *Modus baptizandi* and *Missa* were instead designed to correct European misconceptions. As he explained in the preface to the *Modus baptizandi*, Ethiopian Christianity was now viewed with suspicion and even judged heretical, "even though our people have stood with the shield of truth in the way of this long divulged false opinion." His new Latin translations would likewise "stand in the way of this so great a lie," even if "it is of little or no importance the observance of different ceremonies, as long as it [i.e., the observance] all agrees in one faith."[219] This ecumenicalism underpins both editions: the translated baptism ritual challenged the allegation of an Ethiopian baptism by fire and branding, while the translated missal demonstrated the points of similarity between the Catholic and Ethiopian Orthodox liturgies, even as it deviated from the Ge'ez text of the Nicene Creed and reduced the number of Ethiopian saints named in the Divine Praises.[220] As Latin works, the *Missa* and *Modus*

---

[215] This framing paralleled the founding narrative of the thirteenth century Church of Lalibela, which reified Ethiopia as the new Zion.

[216] A similar language of renewal informs the royal chronicle of Gälawdéwos.

[217] *TN*, 225r; 2 Kings 17:23.

[218] *TN*, 28v and 225v: "ተስፋ ጽዮን ማልኀዞ" and "ተስፋ ጽዮን ማልኀዞ"; BAV, Vat. Et. 16, 55/61v: "ተስፋ ጽዮን ማልኀዞ." While Alessandro Bausi and Gianfranco Fiaccadori speculate that *malḥazo* might be an an obscure ecclesiastic title (*EA*, Vol. 5, 525), we propose that it combines "መልኀ," which means "uproot" or "throw away," with the suffix "-ኦ," which suggests the condition of being a product of something, for "one who is removed or uprooted." Thus "ተስፋ ጽዮን ማልኀዞ" would be "Täsfa Ṣeyon the Exile," paralleling his earlier self-characterization in this same passage as "አነ ኢትዮጲያዊ ፈለ[ላ]ሲ," or "I, an uprooted Ethiopian," and additionally, the scriptural usage of "መልኀ" in connection to the Israelite condition of exile or uprootedness: for example, Jeremiah 12:14 "ናሁ እነ እመልሖሙ እምነ ምድሮሙ," or "Behold, I will uproot them from their land." This meaning is further suggested by Ludolf, *Lexicon*, 59, which identifies – possibly on the basis of *abba* Gorgoryos's explanation – *malḥazo* as part of Täsfa Ṣeyon's personal name, as opposed to a title, which would typically precede a name.

[219] *Modus baptizandi*, iiv.   [220] Kelly, *Translating Faith*, 250–58.

baptizandi had a wide immediate readership, even if the *Testamentum Novum* proved of more enduring influence.

Three years later, Vittori published *Chaldeae seu Aethiopicae linguae institutiones* (1552), the first printed grammar of an African language. It predates by a century Giacinto Brusciotto's 1659 Kikongo grammar, commonly considered the first work of its kind.[221] Vittori's Ge'ez grammar featured a detailed guide to pronunciation, parts of speech, and verb conjugation, with usage examples in fidäl and frequent comparisons with Hebrew. The work also contains the first overview of Ethiopian liturgical music, and additionally, a translated chronology of Ethiopian kings, which haphazardly jumps from the ancient Queen of Sheba and her son Menilek to the sixteenth-century Lebnä Dengel and Gälawdéwos.[222] With respect to his Ge'ez language skills, Vittori acknowledged his debt to his teacher, noting that Täsfa Şeyon had instructed him "with great benevolence"[223] and encouraged the creation of a grammar geared toward European students, adapting an Ethiopian approach to language instruction (*säwasew*) for a new audience.[224]

Vittori delivered. With respect to language study, he outlined a "new system" for Europeans who wished to learn Ge'ez, which he hoped would facilitate research into "the sacred old authors" whose writings had been "learnedly and eruditely" translated into Ge'ez. At the same time, he intervened in several orientalist debates. In his introduction, he likened the study of Ge'ez to the earlier restoration of Greek and Hebrew as languages of fruitful Christian inquiry and instruments of anti-Protestant polemic, complementing Cervini's strategic vision, and he then ventured that the similarities between ancient Chaldean and Hebrew, Syriac, Arabic, and Ge'ez were so extensive that "whoever is good at one, is able to a great degree to understand the other," despite their grammatical and phonetic differences. However, he confirmed that Ge'ez was not in fact Chaldean, contrary to the claims of Potken and Postel, and then railed against Potken, who "not only did not know the language's grammar" but also was "persuaded by the testimony of some Ethiopian ignoramuses ... [to] believe the language to be without any certain grammatical rules, acquired only through use, through the practice of speaking."[225] Finally, and most broadly, Vittori defended the dignity of Ethiopian Christianity, in a nod to both his teacher and Cervini, Góis, and Şägga Zä'ab. In his view, the study of Ethiopian texts – like Eastern Christian literature more generally – presented the opportunity "to gather and collect from all sides what is good."[226]

---

[221] Brusciotto, *Regulæ*; Fellman, "First Grammar."
[222] Victorius, *Chaldeae*; Shelemay and Jeffery, eds., *Liturgical Chant*, 131–62.
[223] Victorius, *Chaldeae*, unpaginated introduction.
[224] Kelly, "Ethiopian Languages," 349–51.
[225] Victorius, *Chaldeae*, unpaginated introduction.
[226] Victorius, *Chaldeae*, unpaginated introduction.

The volume initially had a limited circulation, but for more than a century, it remained the only Ge'ez grammar available in Europe.[227] For this reason, it was reprinted in 1630 by the Propaganda Fide's Tipografia Poliglotta (Figure 13), at the apex of early modern Catholic missionary activity in Ethiopia. Three quarters of a century after Vittori and Täsfa Ṣeyon produced a learning aid for Europeans seeking to understand Ethiopian texts, their work had mutated into a weaponized missionary grammar of an African language.

4 The Influencer

Alessandro Farnese was the breakthrough star of his clan. Eschewing a military career, the future Pope Paul III studied in Rome and Florence before entering the curia. When his sister's husband Rodrigo Borgia (1431–1503) became Pope Alexander VI in 1492, Alessandro was named cardinal, beginning a long ascent within the Vatican. In 1513, he was appointed Dean of the College of Cardinals, and he began purchasing property around what became Piazza Farnese, where his personal residence rivaled the Apostolic Palace and his entourage became the most extensive of all the cardinals.[228] Finally, in 1534 he was elevated to the papacy as Paul III. He quickly installed his relatives in key positions and energetically moved to address the central challenges of the day, appointing outsiders and reformers to key curial positions, restoring and renovating the recently sacked city, brokering a taut reconciliation with Charles V (1519–58), and launching a coordinated counteroffensive against the Protestants. In the process, he transformed the most powerful institution in Europe.

He was aided in these endeavors by a sprawling network of advisors and aides, the *familia papae*. Like other princely clans and family firms, the Farnese thrived through a shrewd combination of nepotism, patronage, and exogenous assimilation, and as pontiff, he appointed his relatives to key posts. But he also welcomed newcomers to the immense Farnese fold. These included the orientalist-cardinal Contarini as well as the zealous Neapolitan archbishop Giampietro Carafa (1476–1559), the future Pope Paul IV. These were the elite of the papal network of formal and honorary clients, employed within his personal service and installed throughout his administration. Beneath them were hundreds of newly arrived junior agents, from the printer Antonio Blado – the publisher of the *Testamentum Novum* – to the *familia* of the just-deceased Ippolito de' Medici (1511–35).[229]

---

[227] Kelly, "Ethiopian Languages," 351. [228] Gamrath, *Farnese*, 33–35.
[229] Sachet, *Publishing for the Popes*, 35.

ዝንቱ፡ መጽሐፉ፡ ትምህርት፡ ዘልሳነ፡ ግዕዝ፡
ዘይስመይ፡ ከሌዳዊ፡ ሐዲስ፡ ስርአት፡ ተገብረ፡
ከመ፡ ይትመሀሩ፡ እለ፡ ኢየአምሩ፡ ወናይ፡ወእቱ፡
ተገብረ፡ በእደ፡ ማሪኣና፡ ዊቶሪአ፡ ዘሪእቱ።

CHALDEAE,
SEV
AETHIOPICAE
LINGVAE
INSTITVTIONES.
Opus vtile, ac eruditum.

R O M A E,
Typis Sac. Congregationis de Propaganda Fide.
M D C X X X.

SVPERIORVM LICENTIA.

Figure 13 Title page, Mariano Vittori, *Chaldeae, Seu Aethiopicae Linguae Institutiones* (Rome: Congregationis de Propaganda Fide, 1630)

The sinews of these relationships of influence, reciprocity, and control were maintained by the Camera Apostolica. A senior curial office that managed pontifical finances, its Secret Treasury archives document the pope's vast personal network, mapping through accounting ledgers the financial and material transactions that sustained the *familia papae*.[230] These ledgers reveal Paul III's personal relationship with Täsfa Ṣeyon, who received a series of financial and material disbursements at the peak of his curial influence. Notably, a monthly stipend between December 1545 and May 1548[231] enabled Täsfa Ṣeyon to hire a Latin tutor, the Sicilian priest Antonio Lo Duca (1491–1564), whose purpose is suggested by the timing: the payments began the same month as the Council of Trent, and one year before Cervini and Sirleto's exchanges about the translation of Ethiopian liturgy and Ge'ez Nicene canons. This coincidence indicates that Cervini and Sirleto's research into Ethiopian Christianity was at this time already envisioned, in that they understood Täsfa Ṣeyon needed Latin training to produce sound translations. The stipend ended just months before the publication of the *Testamentum Novum*, *Missa*, and *Modus baptizandi*, which featured the fruit of this tutelage. Paul III thus personally sponsored Täsfa Ṣeyon's project of intercultural textual transmission, as noted in the multilingual frontispiece of the *Testamentum Novum*, which displayed the pontiff's coat of arms.

Other Secret Treasury disbursements supported the community at Santo Stefano (Figure 14). This patronage made Täsfa Ṣeyon into a curial intermediary, in that he assumed the functions of the *mäggabi*. In April 1546, he received one *scudo* to purchase a compendium of Catholic guidelines for daily life, and one month later, he was given funds to purchase "eight parchment paper booklets for a missal."[232] The following year, in April 1547, the Secret Treasury disbursed twelve *scudi* "for the tin to print in their language," subsidizing the casting of moveable fidäl type, and in May 1548, the pontiff donated three *scudi* for the return of "some Indian [Ethiopian] friars" to Jerusalem.[233] Finally, when Paul III died the following year, Täsfa Ṣeyon and eleven companions received black cloth for the vestments that would allow them to join the *familia papae* at the pontiff's funeral.[234]

Even after this event, the *mämher* retained his stature in the papal court. The familiar registry of Pope Julius III (1550–55) lists disbursements to

---

[230] Levillain and Blaz, *Papacy*, Vol. 1, 559.
[231] ASR, Camerale 1, Tesoreria Segreta [TS], Registro 1293, 72v, 77r, 79r, 81v, 84r, 87v, 90r, 93v, 95v, 98r, 99r, 104r, 108v, 110v, 116v, 129r, 132r, 136r, 141v, 145v, 148r, 152r, 155v, 161v, 162v, 166v, 172r.
[232] ASR, Camerale 1, TS, Registro 1293, 84r, 87r.
[233] ASR, Camerale 1, TS, Registro 1293, 125r, 173r.
[234] ASR, Camerale I, Giustificazioni Tesoreria, bust. 2, fasc. 7, 13r.

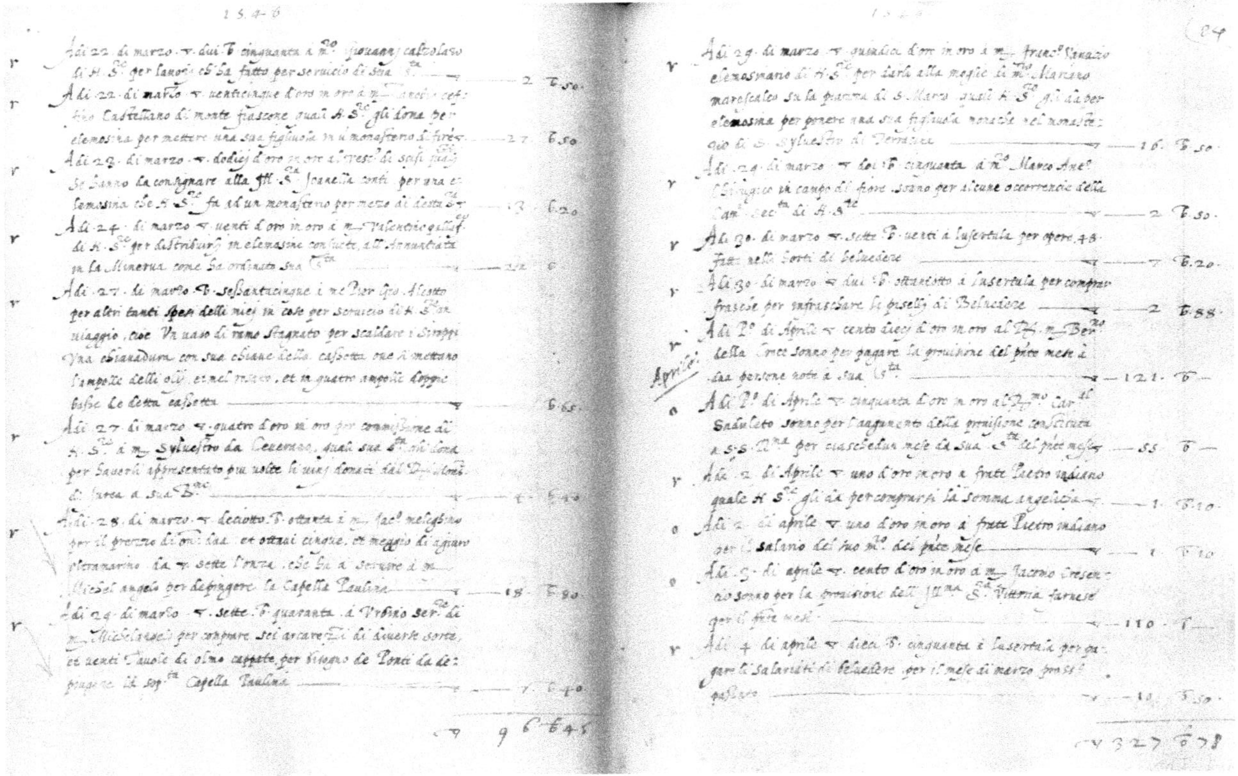

Figure 14 Papal disbursements to Täsfa Ṣeyon, ASR, Camerale I, Registro 1293, 83v–84r – ASR. Aut. prot. 3196-A/2023

Figure 15 Niccolò Circignani, *Ascanio della Corgna receiving a fief from Julius III in 1550*, Palazzo della Corgna, Castiglione del Lago, 1574 (photo by Matteo Burico)

"13 Frati mori Indiani," including "Frate Petro Indiano,"[235] and Täsfa Ṣeyon even appeared with Yoḥannes of Cyprus in a 1574 fresco by Niccolò Circignani called Pomarancio, which depicts the new pontiff granting a fief to his *condottiere* nephew (Figure 15).[236] Cumulatively, these developments suggest the institutionalization of the Vatican link to Santo Stefano.[237] In the decades that

---

[235] ASR, Giustificazioni Tesoreria, bust. 2, fasc. 13, 11r.
[236] It has not been previously noted that this painting depicts Täsfa Ṣeyon as a Black man with a receding hairline, black robe, and white collar, paralleling his depiction in the Gesù painting, discussed later in this section. We thank Cristelle Baskins for bringing the fresco to our attention. Kliemann, *Gesta dipinte*, 91–93.
[237] BAV, Vat. Et. 66, *passim*.

followed, similar transactions formalized Vatican relations with other Eastern Christian populations in Rome, following the Ethiopian precedent established by Paul III.[238]

Far from Däbrä Libanos and the itinerant court of the Ethiopian highlands, Täsfa Ṣeyon had effectively situated himself within the powerful Farnese *kätäma*. This development reflected the curia's interest in Ethiopian texts that could sustain the thesis of Roman supremacy in Trent, and additionally, its desire for a path toward reunification with the Ethiopian church. Yet it was also spurred by Täsfa Ṣeyon himself, in that he actively drew familial interest and support to himself, his companions, and ultimately his distant homeland. The full scope of this agency is demonstrated by his decisive intervention in two endeavors that reached far beyond the walls of the Vatican: the campaign to construct the Basilica of Santa Maria degli Angeli e dei Martiri in Rome, and the conception and dispatch of the first Jesuit mission to Ethiopia.

Antonio Lo Duca and Santa Maria degli Angeli e dei Martiri

Täsfa Ṣeyon's assimilation within the Roman elite is epitomized by his relationship with his Latin teacher Antonio Lo Duca. Their meeting was fortuitous. In 1516, the latter worked at a small Byzantine-era church in Palermo, near the city cathedral.[239] One day, some community members noticed faint images on a wall near the altar, and when these were restored, they revealed a cycle of frescos dedicated to the seven archangels, accompanied by Latinized versions of their Greek names.[240] The church was renamed Chiesa dei Sette Angeli, and devotion to its namesakes exploded such that the city established an archangelic confraternity whose members included Charles V, the king of Sicily since 1516 and Holy Roman emperor after 1519.[241] These developments induced Lo Duca to travel to Rome to research the "Seven Angelic Princes," as he now termed them. In the mid-1520s, he obtained a post with Cardinal Antonio Ciocchi del Monte (1461–1533), uncle of the future Julius III, and he began work on a mass of the archangels, building upon Leo X's 1518 bull establishing the Divine Office of the Guardian Angels.[242] But the project stalled when Paul III rejected the mass, and in 1535, Lo Duca retreated to Palermo, resigned "to finish his life in the church of Santa Croce and never again return to Rome."[243]

---

[238] Santus, "Wandering Lives." [239] BAV, Vat. Lat. 8735, 9r.
[240] Antonio Lo Duca to Lucretia Rovere Colonna, undated, BAV, Vat. Lat. 8735, 9r.
[241] BAV, Vat. Lat. 8735, 12r, 13r. [242] BAV, Vat. Lat. 8735, 15v.
[243] BAV, Vat. Lat. 8735, 18r.

Undaunted, Lo Duca was back in Rome by 1541, still bent on realizing his dream. One summer morning, he experienced a vision:

> I woke up and once awake I immediately stood sitting on my bed, resting on my arms, rigid as a column; I thought myself to be inside the Baths of Diocletian. In the yard in front of the door of the Baths, a light whiter than snow radiated up from the ground of the Baths, shining more than a crystal. It showed me the Baths in a clearer fashion than if I had seen them with my own eyes.[244]

The light revealed that the Baths were "the temple of the seven spirit assistants before God,"[245] and Lo Duca now dedicated himself to the construction of a church in the Baths devoted to the seven archangels and seven Diocletian martyrs.[246] In December 1541, he unsuccessfully proposed the plan to Paul III as well as Margherita of Parma (1522–86), the daughter of Charles V and wife of Duke Ottavio Farnese (1524–86), the pontiff's grandson, and the following year, he failed to win over Cardinal Alessandro Farnese, Ottavio's brother. In 1543, he changed course and ventured to Venice, where he was inspired by "an ancient mosaic depicting the glorious Virgin Mary Mother of God between seven Angels."[247] He printed the first edition of his new mass in the republic, entitled *Septem principum angelorum orationes cum missae eorum antiquis imaginibus* (Figure 16), featuring original woodcuts based on the Palermo frescoes.[248] It was subsequently reprinted in Rome and Naples.

Back in Rome, Lo Duca now renewed his campaign for a church. Its turning point came in 1544–45, when he made a chance but consequential acquaintance. As he told a friend years later, he was hired by "a certain Pietro Indiano to whom he taught Latin for three years."[249] As they worked together between 1545 and 1548, it emerged that Täsfa Ṣeyon could aid the Sicilian in his plans to transform the Diocletian Baths. Although Lo Duca was relatively well-introduced to the Roman curia, his student's reach into its elite – and the preeminent Farnese clan – far exceeded his own. The two engaged this network.

In the later 1540s, Täsfa Ṣeyon took Lo Duca's plan to Vittoria Farnese (1519–1602), the daughter of Girolama Orsini (1504–69) and Pier Luigi Farnese (1503–47), the Duke of Parma and illegitimate son of Paul III. As the Sicilian later explained: "This brother Peter, having easy access to Lady

---

[244] Antonio Lo Duca to Lucretia Rovere Colonna, November 13, 1546, Rome, BAV, Vat. Lat. 8735, 21v.
[245] BAV, Vat. Lat. 8735, 22r. [246] Bernardi Salvetti, *Lo Duca*, 61–67.
[247] BAV, Vat. Lat. 8735, 34v. [248] Duca, *Septem principum angelorum*.
[249] BAV, Vat. Lat. 8735, 35v. This is a manuscript history of the church by Lo Duca's companion Matteo Catalani: Valenziano, "Introduzione."

Figure 16 Title page, Antonio Lo Duca, *Septem principum angelorum orationes cum missae eorum antiquis imaginibus* (Venice: 1543). Biblioteca centrale della Regione siciliana "Alberto Bombace." Palermo. Permission granted by the Dipartimento Beni Culturali e dell'Identità Siciliana

Vittoria ... took the mass of the angels and the prayers with the images that Antonio had printed in Venice and brought them to Lady Vittoria so that she could lobby to build the church in said baths."[250] The premise of this intervention was Täsfa Ṣeyon's clan influence, a proximity memorialized in the *Testamentum Novum*'s dedication to Girolama: "our protector and aide in times of need."[251] Decades later, in 1575, her daughter Vittoria remembered Täsfa Ṣeyon while visiting the Baths with Matteo Catalani (1522–1614), Lo Duca's friend. She recalled the relentless efforts on behalf of its church "by brother Pietro Indiano," which had spurred her own overtures to the pope. Catalani related that on one occasion, Lo Duca even asked his Ethiopian pupil to sneak him in

---

[250] BAV, Vat. Lat. 8735, 36r.   [251] Mauro da Leonessa, *Santo Stefano*, 194.

54   *The Renaissance*

Figure 17 Recaptioned image of the Annunciation of Isaac's Birth, Petrus Ethyops [Täsfa Ṣeyon], *Testamentum Novum cum Epistola Pauli ad Hebreos* [...] (Rome: Valerius Doricus, 1548)

into Paul III's summer residence, in the hopes of directly petitioning the pontiff.[252] Nevertheless, Paul III judged the project too expensive.[253]

Meanwhile, the mutual influence reciprocated. As Täsfa Ṣeyon lobbied for Lo Duca, his *Testamentum Novum* became intertwined with the latter's *Orationes cum missae* through his creative repurposing of Lo Duca's woodcuts.[254] In the *Testamentum Novum,* six of these woodcuts appeared before the Acts of the Apostles, reordered from Lo Duca's sequence and recaptioned with Ge'ez titles featuring the Ethiopian names of the archangels, as distinct from their Latinized counterparts.[255] Separate from this group is a seventh woodcut (Figure 17) that appears after the Book of Revelation, alongside one of Täsfa Ṣeyon's two commentaries on the parallels between ancient Israel and sixteenth-century Ethiopia, discussed in the previous section.[256] The significance of this analogy is deepened by its accompanying woodcut. The image depicts Abraham kneeling and serving cakes to three angelic visitors, who deliver the miraculous news that the elderly Sarah will bear a son, as described in Genesis 18.

---

[252] BAV, Vat. Lat. 8735, 38v–40v.   [253] BAV, Vat. Lat. 8735, 41r.
[254] BAV, Vat. Lat. 8735, 9r–12r.   [255] *TN*, 131v–133v.   [256] *TN*, 113r.

It is a resonant scene. On one level, its depiction of an inspired exile prostrate before God, humbled in the act of service, perhaps parallels the editorial self-imagination of Täsfa Ṣeyon, a similarly displaced pious servant who offered his nourishing gift of the printed word. But on another level, the scene also documents a pivotal historical event. In the Ethiopian Orthodox tradition, the three prophetic visitors are not archangels but the Holy Trinity of Abraham, or *abrehamu śellasé*. In this appearance, then, "the masters"[257] of the Trinity, as Täsfa Ṣeyon rechristened them in the Ge'ez caption to the woodcut, announced the birth of Isaac, the lineal progenitor of the Israelites. When seen in this aspect, the image can be understood as depicting the precise origin moment of the Solomonid dynasty. Read in tandem with the accompanying Ge'ez text, the woodcut thus affirms the lineage of Gälawdéwos – the living heir of Abraham, Sarah, and Isaac – and metaphorically suggests a similarly miraculous revival of their imperiled dynasty. Täsfa Ṣeyon specifically noted this link in the Latin preface to the *Testamentum Novum*, where he identified Abraham as the ancestor of the Solomonids.[258] These connections would have been clear to a learned Ethiopian reader, but were likely unknown to Lo Duca, who had commissioned the original woodcut.

The Sicilian also learned from his Ethiopian pupil. In 1555, he issued a new edition of his mass, but his envisioned church renovation was not supported by popes Marcello Cervini (1555) and Paul IV (1555–59). Pius IV (1559–65), however, proved receptive, and in 1561, he approved Lo Duca's plan for the Baths. Despite this endorsement, the project still faced resistance. Unnamed members of the curia now objected on doctrinal grounds because "some of the names of the seven Angels were new and as such they could not be received."[259] Specifically, four of Lo Duca's archangels were mentioned only in Catholic apocrypha, and for this reason, the schema diverged from the Tridentine climate of rigid scripturalism. Put simply, the Byzantine origins of Lo Duca's vision were disquieting.

To settle the matter, the pontiff asked the priest to defend the Seven Angelic Princes. In 1562, Lo Duca filed a memorandum that outlined his position. He explained that the seven archangels were identified in the Palermo frescos as well as the mosaic in Venice. While only the names of Michael, Gabriel, and Raphael appear in the Old Testament and Gospels, the other archangels are indirectly referenced in Revelations as well as the Book of Tobit, and for this reason were broadly supported by the Catholic canon. In an unexpected twist, Lo Duca then offered that the identities of the Seven Angels were well

---

[257] "አጋእዝት"
[258] *TN*, unpaginated Latin introduction; cf. *Modus baptizandi*, unpaginated preface.
[259] BAV, Vat. Lat. 8735, 102r.

attested in the Ethiopian tradition. He invoked "the authority of a certain Abate Giorgio, considered a holy man in Ethiopia," and explained that "[in a] book he wrote to worship the Most Blessed Virgin Mary, entitled *Door of Light*, it is said: 'Veniant Angeli tui Principes de excelso,' etc."[260] The abbot in question is Saint Giyorgis of Sägla (ca. 1365–ca.1425),[261] an eminent Ethiopian theologian and author of the influential *Anqäṣä berhan*, or *Gate of Light*, a collection of Ge'ez hymns to Mary that is chanted alongside the Psalms in the Ethiopian Orthodox liturgy, and which contains a passage very similar to the one cited by Lo Duca, though it does not name specific archangels.[262] A codex containing the *Anqäṣä berhan* was at that time in the Santo Stefano library, and it was briefly excerpted in the 1513 Tomas-Potken Psalter.[263]

After this unexpected gesture to Ethiopian church literature, Lo Duca continued his defense in kind. He next argued that his conception of the Seven Angels also rested on "the authority of a very ancient Chaldean [Ge'ez] book" owned by Yoḥannes of Cyprus, who was "the pope's interpreter."[264] According to Lo Duca, this second Ethiopian work contained a plea to God to "[s]end to us the seven holy archangels together with the swords with their fire which make all unclean spirits depart which surround our body."[265] This referent text is less certain. A likely candidate is the *Dersanä mika'él*, a famous collection of twelve homilies honoring the archangel Mika'él that names the seven archangels of the Ethiopian tradition, and which was possibly among the Ge'ez "books of the church" in the Santo Stefano library.[266] Left unstated by Lo Duca, however, was the potentially compromising fact that the scriptural basis of the *Dersanä mika'él* and *Anqäṣä berhan* – and indeed Ethiopian angelology more broadly – was the Book of Enoch, a canonical work for the Ethiopian church that was considered apocryphal by Catholics.[267] Though the subject of extensive Ethiopian commentary, Enoch was at that time only known to Europeans through its quotation in other languages – a situation that led Postel to Santo Stefano decades before.[268]

Lo Duca could only have understood Ethiopian angelology through Täsfa Ṣeyon and his companions. Given the limited European understanding of Ethiopian Orthodox doctrine and literature, there was no other possible source for a detailed introduction to its angelic esoterica, let alone appropriate

---

[260] BAV, Vat. Lat. 8735, 103v.   [261] *EA*, Vol. 2, 812.
[262] *Anqäṣä berhan*, 4; Derat, *Domaine des rois*. Cf. *EA*, Vol. 1, 278–79.
[263] BAV, Vat. Et. 66, 54v; Potken and Tomas Wäldä Samu'él, *Psalterium*, with ṣälotä maryam on unpaginated final page.
[264] BAV, Vat. Lat. 8735, 103v.   [265] BAV, Vat. Lat. 8735, 103v.   [266] BAV, Vat. Et. 66, 2v.
[267] Daniel Assefa, "Uriel."   [268] Wilkinson, *Orientalism*; Busi and Ebgi, *Pico della Mirandola*.

translations from relevant Ge'ez texts. Although Lo Duca's dedication to the Seven Angelic Princes predated his encounter with Täsfa Ṣeyon, it seems possible that his introduction to the broadly complimentary aspects of Ethiopian angelology would have deepened his conviction in the significance of his vision. His Byzantine orientation opened him to other Eastern Christian traditions, paralleling the intellectual impetus behind the era's *philologia sacra*-based approach to investigating Orthodox texts. Considered from the other side of this exchange, perhaps Täsfa Ṣeyon aided Lo Duca in order to defend the authority of Ethiopian church literature via a Catholic proxy. After all, the Sicilian mystic raised the names of important Ethiopian texts at the highest levels of the curia.

Täsfa Ṣeyon's role in the establishment of the Basilica of Santa Maria degli Angeli e dei Martiri was eventually commemorated in its visual adornments. After Lo Duca submitted his defence of the Seven Angels, Michelangelo Buonarroti (1475–1564) designed its plan, and construction began in 1562.[269] Both Michelangelo and Lo Duca died shortly thereafter, in 1564, but the work continued until the end of the century.[270] In a gesture to this history, the Basilica's Catalani Chapel features a painting titled "Personaggi in Ginocchio," attributed to Giulio Mazzoni (1525–1618) and dedicated to its founding personalities.[271] In addition to Lo Duca, its subjects include Pius IV; Charles V; Cardinal Giovanni Antonio Serbelloni (1519–91), the church's titular cardinal; Bishop Filippo Archinto, Rome's Vicar General; brothers Antonio and Domenico Massimo, a Roman Conservator and the Capitano Generale della Chiesa, respectively; and Margherita d'Austria, together with Alessandro Farnese, Vittoria Farnese, and Girolama Farnese.[272] Many of these were members of the Fratelli and Sorelle della Confraternita dei Sette Angeli di Roma, the new confraternity dedicated to Lo Duca's archangels. Standing discreetly within the main group is a youthful Täsfa Ṣeyon, his eyes reverently looking down. His inclusion in this founders' painting is a stunning visual confirmation of his standing among the sixteenth-century Roman elite.[273]

Ignatius of Loyola and the Jesuit Mission to Ethiopia

As these events unfolded in Rome, another momentous group gathered in Paris. In 1534, Ignatius of Loyola and six companions founded the Society of Jesus, a new religious order whose members became known to the world as Jesuits. Three years later, in 1537, the Spanish priest arrived in Rome and pledged himself to Paul III, laying the foundation for the formal establishment of the preeminent Counter-

---

[269] According to a *breve* dated 10 March 1562: Valenziano, "Introduzione," 160.
[270] Matthiae, *S. Maria degli Angeli*, 29–31.
[271] Bernardi Salvetti, *Lo Duca*, 83; Pugliatti, *Mazzoni*, 204.
[272] Bernardi Salvetti, *Lo Duca*, 123–42.   [273] Bernardi Salvetti, *Lo Duca*, 178–82.

Figure 18 Anonymous, *Pope Paul III hands Ignatius the Regimini Militantis Ecclesiae on 27 September 1540*, Chiesa del Gesù, Rome (photo by Zeno Colantoni)

Reformation instrument of global salvific Catholicism.[274] The pontiff approved the Society in 1540, as commemorated in a seventeenth-century painting in the Chiesa del Gesù, the Jesuit mother church in Rome (Figure 18).[275] The image depicts Ignatius and four companions kneeling before Paul III, as assorted curial personalities look on. It is a founding moment immortalized in countless paintings, but only the Gesù version includes Täsfa Ṣeyon.[276] He stands immediately behind Paul III, gesturing to Ignatius while whispering in the ear of Archinto, who is similarly at his side in the painting at Santa Maria degli Angeli e dei Martiri.[277] The only other figure in similar proximity to the pontiff is Alessandro Farnese, Paul III's nephew. This inclusion attests to Täsfa Ṣeyon's pivotal role in the establishment of the Jesuit mission to Ethiopia, itself a turning point in the history of the Solomonid kingdom and its relations with the wider world.[278]

---

[274] Clossey, *Jesuit Missions*, 1–19.
[275] On the painting cycle, see Wolk-Simon, "Finger of God."
[276] Salvadore, *Heart of Prester John*.   [277] Bernardi Salvetti, *Lo Duca*, 38.
[278] Martínez d'Alós-Moner, *Envoys*.

Over the course of the 1540s, Ignatius planned the overseas enterprise of his new Society, seeking patrons and identifying fruitful mission regions. Rome was an ideal site for this strategic work, with its curial apparatus, foreign *nationes*, and flow of informed visitors. The city hosted the Society's central offices, including the Superior General, a lifetime position of authority occupied by Ignatius until his death, as well as the Procurator General, the Society's representative at the papal court. No less significant was Lisbon, the metropole of the sprawling global network of Portuguese colonies. In 1540, founding Jesuits Francis Xavier (1506–52) and Simão Rodrigues (1510–79) reached the city and laid the foundation for the Portuguese Province (1546), prefiguring the creation of provinces throughout the empire.[279] All these were coordinated by the Portuguese Assistancy, which encompassed the empire as well as the regions ascribed to Portugal by the treaties of Tordesillas (1494) and Saragossa (1529), through which the Iberian monarchies apportioned the world among themselves, with the blessing of the pontiff.

These evolving geopolitics of empire led the Jesuits to Ethiopia. One agent of this development was Rodrigues. The Portuguese provincial had known of the Solomonid kingdom since his time in Padua, where in the 1530s he had clashed with Góis, who he accused of heresy for corresponding with Martin Luther (1483–1546) and Philip Melancthone (1497–1560), who were themselves in dialogue with an Ethiopian deacon named Mika'él.[280] Góis had at that time already befriended Ṣägga Zä'ab and published his *Legatio* (1532). Now in Lisbon, Rodrigues continued to monitor Góis: he repeatedly denounced his nemesis to the Portuguese Inquisition, and in the process dissected his writings, which now included the *Fides* and its summary of Ṣägga Zä'ab's heretical confession of faith. Given his position at court, Rodrigues was likely privy to the Bermudes controversy as well as the stern letter of Cardinal-Infante Afonso (1509–40), which urged Lebnä Dengel "to conform to the Holy Church and to obey, in all things, the Catholic faith and the Holy Apostolic faith."[281]

All this complemented the interests of Francis Xavier. After establishing himself in the Portuguese court and winning the support of Martin Alfonso de Sousa (1500–64), the Viceroy of the Estado da India, the Spaniard departed for Goa in 1542.[282] The so-called Rome of Asia underpinned the Portuguese Assistancy through its role as the capital of the Estado, in which capacity it

---

[279] Clossey, *Jesuit Missions*, 23.
[280] Hirsch, *De Gois*, 96; Daniels III and Anglin, "Ethiopian Deacon."
[281] Cardinal Alfonso to Emperor Lebnä Dengel, March 20, 1539, Lisbon, in Beccari, *Rerum Aethiopicarum*, Vol. 10, 5–17.
[282] O'Malley, *First Jesuits*, 76.

was the staging ground for Portuguese intelligence and interventions throughout the Indian Ocean arena, including the developing proxy war with Adal and the Ottomans in the Horn.[283] Francis Xavier heard about the Solomonid kingdom from the city's merchants and sizeable Ethiopian community,[284] and in 1544, he informed a companion that he wished to visit "the land of the Preste[r]."[285] This would appear to be the first Jesuit reference to Ethiopia. Given the Society's positions in Rome, Lisbon, and Goa, the three cities upon which Ethiopian–European relations then hinged, as well as the context of the just-dispatched Portuguese garrisons in Ethiopia and the recent controversies involving Sägga Zä'ab, Góis, and Bermudes, it is no surprise that Francis Xavier's vision of a mission to the highlands soon became a Jesuit priority.

This development was furthered by Ignatius's interest in Ethiopia. Broadly, this awareness reflected the wider European intellectual preoccupation with Prester John, and possibly the Jesuit's visits to cities with Ethiopian diaspora populations, including Jerusalem. More concretely, he had intervened in the dispute between Rodrigues and Góis, and was thus familiar with the latter's Ethiopianist work.[286] The first certain glimpse of Ignatius's awareness of Ethiopia appears in a 1546 letter from Salmeron, dispatched to the Jesuit leader from the deliberations at Trent.[287] In it, the Spaniard replied to his superior's queries about the Bermudes controversy. João III had recently moved to appoint a Jesuit Patriarch of Ethiopia, and had even requested Paul III's approval of French theologian Pierre Favre (1506–46) for this office – a scheme that collapsed with the death of the nominee.[288] To properly brief Ignatius on the current state of affairs, Salmeron queried Cervini, who had dealt with the Bermudes curial inquiry before leaving for Trent. In Salmeron's reply to Ignatius, he outlined the events of Bermudes's arrival in Rome, his request for confirmation as the Patriarch of Alexandria, and the critical evaluation of this story by Täsfa Ṣeyon. Salmeron further reported that after this episode Bermudes had returned to Ethiopia, where he falsely claimed that Paul III had confirmed him as patriarch after learning of his appointment as *abun*. Ethiopian pilgrims then brought news of this development to Jerusalem, which led the city's perplexed Catholics to inquire about the situation to Rome.

---

[283] Alden, *Society of Jesus*, 8–28; Clossey, *Jesuit Missions*, 22–30.
[284] Pescatello, "African Presence"; Salvadore, "Slave Trade," 339–43.
[285] Martínez d'Alós-Moner, *Envoys of a Human God*, 42.   [286] Hirsch, *De Gois*, 96.
[287] Salmeron, *Epistolae*, 33–36.
[288] João III to Balthasar de Faria, August 27, 1546, Lisbon, in Silva, *Corpo diplomatico Portuguez*, Vol. 6, 69–72; Pennec, *Jésuites*, 50–51.

This interregional exchange produced a potentially compromising interconfessional predicament. As Salmeron informed Ignatius:

> This matter was sent to I know not how many cardinals, among which to the most reverend Sancta Cruz [Cervini] who says they found that he [Bermudes] had not been elected, nor consecrated, and that he had taken no letters on such matter.... On the one hand, it seemed wrong that an usurper [Bermudes] and a false pastor should be tolerated; on the other hand, removing him and placing another one would cause a great scandal. ... He was the first to have entered in title on behalf of the Apostolic See.... It was then deliberated that ... a bishop should be sent as an emissary to Prester John, so as to determine if that patriarch [Bermudes] led a good life and if he performed the functions of a pastor and, if such was the case, that he would confirm him without rumours or scandal; [otherwise] it would be left to the discretion of the envoy whether he should be removed, corrected, confirmed or if another one should be created.[289]

In short, Bermudes might have been an impostor, but the curia was prepared to ignore this inconvenience in the name of ecumenical expediency, hoping to salvage the potential precedent of a Latin metropolitan appointed by Rome rather than Alexandria. But the politicking was pointless. Cervini, Ignatius, and Salmeron could not know that Bermudes had failed to convince upon his return to Ethiopia, where his claim to the office of *abun* was refused by Gälawdéwos. Meanwhile, the Patriarch of Alexandria dispatched *abunä* Yosab as the new Egyptian metropolitan of the Ethiopian church.[290]

For Ignatius, the entire situation suggested that Ethiopia was ripe for mission. Seeking to learn more in the context of João III's request for a Jesuit Patriarch, he contacted Täsfa Ṣeyon, who had just intervened in Bermudes affair. Santo Stefano was in fact only a short walk from the Chiesa del Gesù, and at some point after receiving Salmeron's 1546 correspondence, Ignatius met its most famous resident. The ex-Jesuit Postel had just preceded him. The Spaniard described his conversations with the Ethiopian in a 1549 letter to a fellow Jesuit, there outlining his developing thoughts about "Prester John." These reflected his consultation with "a friar named Piedro ... [who] leads an honest life and tells many things about those lands ... [and] is credited among cardinals and other prelates."[291] According to Ignatius, the two shared a broadly complimentary vision of Ethiopia's future. He reported that upon learning of the death of the would-be patriarch Favre, Täsfa Ṣeyon

---

[289] Salmeron, *Epistolae*, 33–36.   [290] *EA*, Vol. 1, 540; Solomon Gebreyes, *Gälawdewos*, 201.
[291] Ignatius of Loyola to Ludovico de Grana, January 17, 1549, Rome, in Ignatius of Loyola, *Monumenta Ignatiana*, Vol. 2, 304–308.

soon began to explain the great [spiritual] need of the lands of Prester John ...
and putting his efforts together with those of others, they [Täsfa Ṣeyon and
this group] achieved what they intended, namely, that five bishops would go
to Ethiopia and that Prester John would then elect one of them as patriarch.
[But] Having Lord Pero Luis [Pier Luigi Farnese] died in that time, they did
not have the resources at hand to readily fulfill the expedition.[292]

In other words, Täsfa Ṣeyon had already lobbied the pontiff to send a mission to Ethiopia prior to meeting the Jesuit founder. The proposed plan was revolutionary from an ecclesiastical perspective, in that it circumvented the authority of the Coptic See of Saint Mark in Alexandria. Yet it also gestured to precedent in its practicality: the five Catholic bishops, like the Egyptian bishops that typically accompanied the new Coptic metropolitan, could be imagined as similarly replenishing the ranks of the Ethiopian church hierarchy, then weakened by the Adal invasion and the 1530 death of *abunä* Marqos. The sponsor of this plan was Pier Luigi Farnese, the Duke of Parma whose wife Girolama or daughter Vittoria was likely the planned pontifical intercessor(s). Indeed, both were then already involved in the *Testamentum Novum* and Lo Duca campaign. But Pier Luigi's 1547 assassination stalled Täsfa Ṣeyon's missionary plans, leaving him without a patron and at the mercy of the skeptical Portuguese.

This setback produced a timely alliance. As Ignatius explained,

Friar Piedro, realizing that his intents were hindered, told me the story of his
appointment in the way I have told you (which was not visible to us before,
during the time of his proceedings [i.e., his involvement in the planned
mission]), moving me so that he could go in the company of the patriarch
to be elected by the King, and that, since he knew the languages spoken here
and there etc.; so they could help in such a journey.[293]

From this report, it would seem that a frustrated Täsfa Ṣeyon shared his Ezra-esque vision for regenerating Ethiopian Christianity with the Jesuit, who found the plan and its architect compelling. Ignatius judged the Ethiopian's tenacity a virtue, given the Portuguese hostility: "Friar Piedro ... will make all the possible proceedings in order to achieve his intent," and "Balesar de Faria [the obstructionist Portuguese ambassador] will not have the strength to resist it,"[294] unless the Portuguese monarch could offer an alternative plan to the pontiff. This assessment suggests the tremendous political and curial clout of Täsfa Ṣeyon. In Ignatius's estimation, the powerful Portuguese ambassador was no match for the Farnese's Ethiopian *mämher*.

---

[292] Ignatius of Loyola, *Monumenta Ignatiana*, Vol. 2, 304.
[293] Ignatius of Loyola, *Monumenta Ignatiana*, Vol. 2, 305.
[294] Ignatius of Loyola, *Monumenta Ignatiana*, Vol. 2, 305.

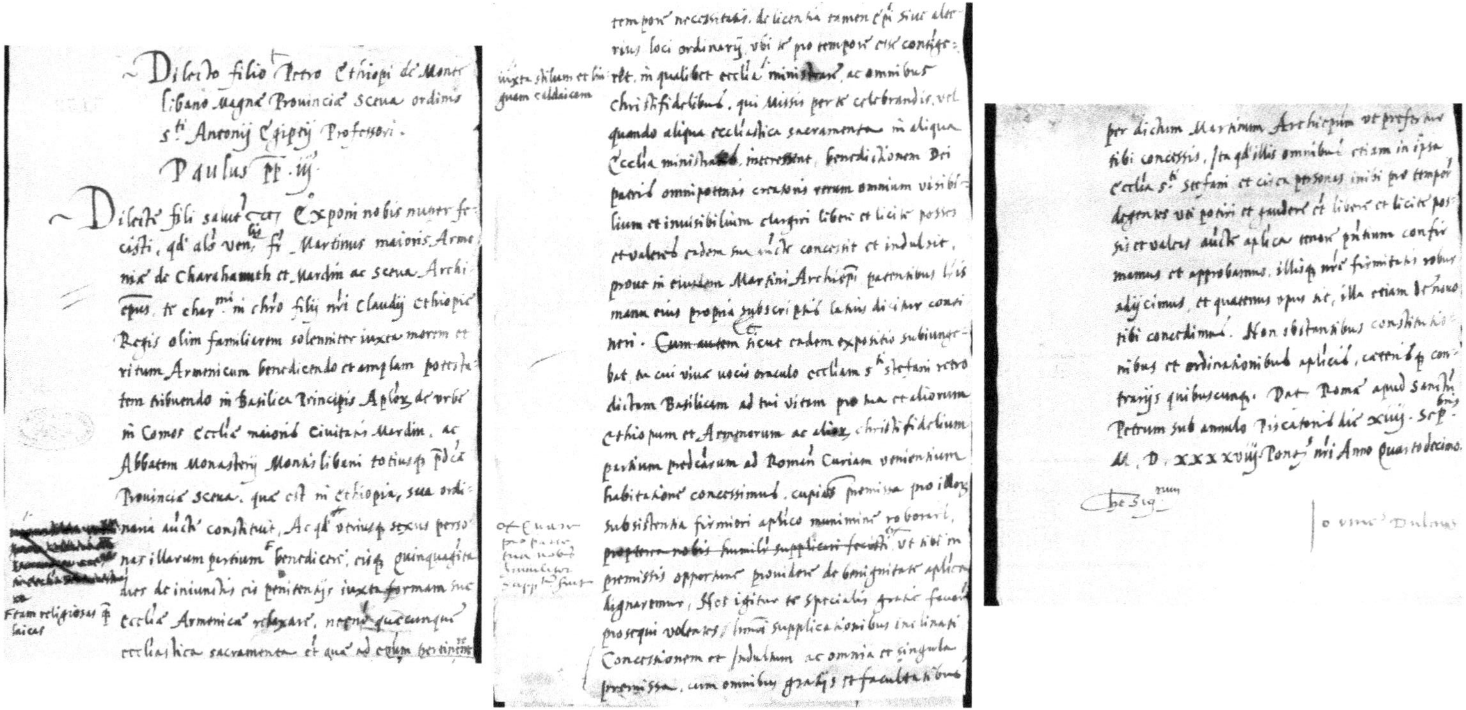

Figure 19 Paul III to Täsfa Ṣeyon, September 4, 1548, Rome, Dataria Apostolica, Min. Brev. Lat., AAV, 1548, n. 8152

The Jesuit's motivations parallel Täsfa Ṣeyon's own activities in this same period. In 1548, Paul III addressed a papal brief to his "beloved son" Täsfa Ṣeyon, the first brief by any pope directed to an Ethiopian. The document confusingly acknowledged Täsfa Ṣeyon's elevation as "abbot of the monastery of Mount Lebanon [Däbrä Libanos] and the entire ... province of Shäwa" by the visiting Armenian Archbishop Martiros. The pontiff confirmed this surprising development as well as Täsfa Ṣeyon's "apostolic authority," additionally designating Santo Stefano "as habitation for you, the other Ethiopians and Armenians" (Figure 19).[295] One year later, the visiting Armenian Patriarch Stephanos V issued another attestation to Täsfa Ṣeyon, in which he thanked him for serving as his interpreter, and obliquely referred to the *mämher*'s appointment as archbishop of "the district of Malhzua ... in the land with its own province and on his see of Faraka."[296] The Armenian language references to Ge'ez and/or Amharic terms are confused, but the document appears to establish Täsfa Ṣeyon's ecclesiastic authority over the "uprooted" Ethiopian and Armenian pilgrims in Rome, as suggested by the Ge'ez *malḥazo*, as well as their coreligionists in Africa, here indicated through an apparent corruption of the Amharic *afriqa* or possibly the Arabic *'ifrīqīya*.

As the fate of the Ethiopian mission hung in the balance, Täsfa Ṣeyon mobilized his proximity to Rome's Armenian community to obtain interconfessional credentials that bolstered his chance of joining the inchoate Jesuit delegation, possibly as one of its bishops. It hardly seems a coincidence that during this same period Täsfa Ṣeyon edited, financed, and published the *Testamentum Novum*, addressed to his suffering religious brethren in "Mother Ethiopia." As a mass printed text, it would have been a revolutionary salvific instrument, leaving aside the central and essential question of whether Ethiopia's future spiritual revival would take an Orthodox or Catholic form. He even printed personalized versions for Paul III (Figure 12), Charles V, Henry II of France, and cardinals Cervini, Ciocchi Da Monte, Ranuccio Farnese (1530–65), Reginald Pole, Juan Alvarez de Toledo (1488–1557), and Nicolò Ridolfi (1501–50), likely in an effort to obtain more patrons for his plan.[297] In 1549, when Täsfa Ṣeyon exhorted the Vatican conclavists to elect Cardinal Francesco Sfrondati (1493–1550), he even "promis[ed] he [himself] would give

---

[295] Paul III to Täsfa Ṣeyon, September 4, 1548, Rome, AAV, Dataria Apostolica, Min. Brev. Lat., 1548, n. 8152.
[296] Ališan, Հայապատում, 592–93; see also Petrowicz, *Patriarca di Ecimiazin*, 366.
[297] Fumagalli, *Bibliografia etiopica*, 131; Lefevre, "Tasfa Seyon," 88.

obedience in the name of the Ethiopian Church."[298] His sudden death cut short these bold designs.

Meanwhile, Ignatius went on to develop the strategic framework for the Jesuit mission to Ethiopia. Drawing upon his conversations with Täsfa Ṣeyon as well as Álvares's just-published *Ho Preste Ioam das Indias*, the first detailed European account of Ethiopian Christianity, he issued a series of 1553–56 directives that reveal his sophisticated yet ultimately flawed understanding of Ethiopian religious dynamics. At bottom, Ignatius misjudged the close – albeit occasionally rocky – relationship between the Solomonid church and state, and fundamentally misread the receptiveness of the Ethiopian faithful to Catholic evangelism. These positions reflected Ignatius's analysis of recent European contacts with Ethiopia, and more specifically, his conclusions from his own consultation with Täsfa Ṣeyon.

It is easy to imagine the *mämher*'s testimony informing the Spaniard's focus on converting influential Ethiopian ecclesiastics and court advisors, who could aid the ultimate goal of converting a Solomonid monarch. If this top-down strategy characterized the general Jesuit approach to mission, in the Ethiopian setting it hinged upon the dynamics of an elite world that Täsfa Ṣeyon knew well, and which Ignatius barely understood. Whatever the *mämher*'s specific views, their dialogue provided evidence for the Spaniard's preestablished position on Jesuit strategy. Equally plausible is the possibility that Täsfa Ṣeyon's concern for the calamitous impact of the Adal invasion supported Ignatius's claim that the struggle with "the Moors" would make Ethiopian Christians receptive to the messages of their foreign coreligionists. Both the Ethiopian and the Spaniard imagined an existential spiritual crisis. More certain than these speculative points is the fact that Täsfa Ṣeyon's sophisticated ecumenism and Santo Stefano's accommodating monastic culture jointly buttressed Ignatius's position that the Ethiopian populace and clergy might welcome interconfessional overtures and Catholic conversion. This fundamental error conflated the diasporic particularity of the Jesuit's Ethiopian contacts in Rome with the altogether different institutional religious politics in the Horn. Inherent in his position was the irresolvable contradiction of "evangelizing the evangelized."[299] The Spaniard saw Ethiopian Christianity as a lost child of Rome rather than a bastion of the true faith, casting its resilient elaboration of Christianity as spiritual deficiency and ignorant

---

[298] According to Pietro Paolo Gualtieri's diary, in Merkle, *Concilium Tridentinum*, Vol. 2, 87.
[299] Taddesse Tamrat, "Root Problem."

superstition. Generations of later missionaries embraced this Eurocentric vision.

In 1555, the first Jesuits reached Ethiopia. It proved one of the Society's earliest overseas missions, and among its most disastrous. From the Jesuits' first visit to Gälawdéwos (1540–59) through their 1632 ejection from the court of Fasilädas (1632–67), the missionaries worked relentlessly yet ineffectively to Catholicize Ethiopia. As Ignatius's flawed directives failed to yield progress, some Jesuits proposed more aggressive forms of mission. In 1556, one petitioned the Estado for a Jesuit military escort, and in 1563, another suggested that an envoy of Portuguese soldiers could aid the goal of driving away "the Turks" and "introducing the Catholic faith."[300] In 1567, Patriarch Oviedo begged for a military expedition as "[the] great hope of bringing back these lands to the union with the Catholic faith and of converting the heathens."[301] Even when Emperor Susenyos (1607–32) converted to Catholicism in 1621, it did not trigger the mass Catholicization Ignatius envisioned, but instead provoked a period of interconfessional violence that only ceased when the emperor abdicated in favor of his Orthodox son Fasilädas. The latter's subsequent expulsion of the Jesuits proved a major embarrassment for the Catholic Church. This failure reflected the founder's gross misinterpretation of Ethiopian Christianity, even if the calls for militarized mission deviated from Ignatius's original strategy. It was the first of Täsfa Ṣeyon's many unexpected legacies.

5 Rediscoveries

After more than a decade in Rome, Täsfa Ṣeyon fell ill. At some point in 1549 or early 1550, he relocated to the hilltop town of Tivoli, presumably to benefit from its restorative thermal springs. He died there in 1552.[302] His brothers in faith interred him at Santo Stefano, where they inscribed his bilingual epitaph on a marble plaque (Figure 20):

> [Ge'ez] Here is buried the Ethiopian priest Täsfa Ṣeyon. Commemorate him through your holy prayers and offerings for the sake of the Christ and the mother of Christ. Amen.
> [Latin] Tzafa Zior Malbazo [Täsfa Ṣeyon Malḫazo] Ethiopian pilgrim by the name of Pietro, born beyond the Capricorn circle from noble parents, fluent in many languages, well read in the sacred scriptures, welcomed by Europeans of every status, extremely charitable toward men of every nationality. After having lived in Jerusalem near the grave of Christ he came to

---

[300] Pennec, *Jésuites*, 99.
[301] Beccari, *Rerum Aethiopicarum*, Vol. 10, 215–20, 332–34; Vol. 3, 71–75; and Vol. 5, 427–32.
[302] Euringer, "Tasfa Sejon."

Figure 20 Täsfa Ṣeyon's epitaph, date unknown, Santo Stefano degli Abissini, Vatican City (photo by the author)

> Rome where, enjoying great favor, he obtained a dwelling for the convenience of pilgrims from his country, and he edited, with great difficulty and expense, the printing of the New Testament in Ethiopic[,] and the ritual that the Ethiopians use for baptism and the Ethiopian mass translated into Latin. While he was busy with great things that would have been useful to all of Ethiopia and which [he] would have been able to accomplish had he survived, [he was] struck by a long illness, [and] in Tivoli, where due to his illness he retired, he died on 28 August 1550 [sic].[303]

At this sepulchral memory site, the life and death of Täsfa Ṣeyon were defining community events.

Nearly five centuries later, in 2020, Pope Francis celebrated the centenary of the Pontifical Ethiopian College, the modern successor of Santo Stefano and the only African seminary within the Vatican.[304] Addressing a large audience at the Apostolic Palace, the pontiff observed that the history of "the Ethiopian presence within the Vatican walls" exemplified the universality of the church, echoing the internationalist spirit of the Second Vatican Council (1962–65). This connection rested, in his judgment, upon a single word: *accoglienza*, or "hospitality." Beyond the individual reciprocity of host and guest, the word invoked Francis's vision of realizing authentic ecumenical and interreligious dialogue, reconciliation, and atonement, achieved in part by recognizing the dignity of non-Western Christians. This spirit, Francis continued, was

---

[303] See Online Appendix Item 5.   [304] Sala Stampa della Santa Sede, "Udienza."

epitomized by Täsfa Ṣeyon. He read the latter's words to the assembly, quoting the Latin conclusion of the *Testamentum Novum*:

> I myself am Ethiopian, a pilgrim from place to place ... but nowhere, except in Rome, have I found peace of mind and body: peace of mind because here is the true faith; peace of body, because here I have found the Successor of Peter, who provides for our needs.[305]

For the pontiff, Täsfa Ṣeyon exemplified his country's enduring contributions to the universal church. Like their sixteenth-century forebear, contemporary Ethiopian and Eritrean Catholics were stewards of one of the world's oldest Christian traditions, and were models of interconfessional fraternity and hospitality in an era of conflict. For Francis, the human suffering of the contemporary Horn paralleled the conditions that had impelled Täsfa Ṣeyon and countless others to leave their ancestral home, "at enormous cost and effort" and often through "tragedies on land and at sea." This was a timely reference given the ongoing work of the diasporic Catholic priest *abba* Mussé Zär'ay to rescue detained and trafficked Eritrean, Ethiopian, and Sudanese migrants across the Mediterreanean.[306] Against this contemporary backdrop, Francis judged Täsfa Ṣeyon an exemplar of the enduring hardship of displacement and the salvific and liberatory power of true ecumenism. He was an avatar of the modern predicament. How did such an imagination come about?

Orientalist Translations

Täsfa Ṣeyon entered the modern academy via two Germans. The first was Hiob Ludolf (1624–1704), a linguist and historian widely considered among the founders of the academic field of Ethiopian studies (Figure 21). Trained in Erfurt and Leiden, Ludolf was an admirer of Eastern Christianity and accomplished student of Semitic languages, including Ge'ez, Syriac, and Arabic.[307] His Ethiopia-focused research developed from a diplomatic mission to Rome, where he began an extended collaboration with *abba* Gorgoryos (nd–1658), a Catholic ex-advisor of Emperor Susenyos who arrived at Santo Stefano after the Jesuit expulsion from Ethiopia (Figure 22). Their partnership yielded several major publications, including a monumental two-part history of Ethiopia as well as a series of groundbreaking Ge'ez and Amharic dictionaries and grammars.[308]

---

[305] *TN*, 226rv, with the corresponding Ge'ez passage on 225rv.
[306] On this, see the website of Agenzia Habeshia: https://habeshia.blogspot.com/p/about.html.
[307] *EA*, Vol. 3, 601–3; Hamilton, *Copts and the West*, 140–57.
[308] Ludolf, *Grammatica*; Ludolf, *Lexicon*, 1661; Ludolf, *Historia*; Ludolf, *Commentarius*.

Figure 21 Hiob Ludolf in Hiob Ludolf, *Iobi Ludolfi Ad Suam Historiam Aethiopicam Antehac Editam Commentarius* (Frankfurt am Main: Zunner, 1691) (photo by the author)

Täsfa Ṣeyon hides in the margins of this oeuvre.[309] Ludolf began his Ge'ez study with the extant Ethiopianist library, including the works of Täsfa Ṣeyon and his students, and his self-taught language skills impressed *abba* Gorgoryos during their first encounter at Santo Stefano, where Ludolf passed a Ge'ez test before the residents. The examination included scripture translation, which tempts one to imagine queries based on the *Testamentum Novum*.[310] More certain, however, is that Täsfa Ṣeyon's publications shaped Ludolf's ensuing scholarship, paralleling the influence of Gorgoryos's instruction. This connection began with Ludolf's *Lexicon Aethiopico-Latinum* (1661), a Ge'ez–Latin dictionary that features illustrative usages throughout via Gospel citations, effective references to the *editio princeps*. These transformed Täsfa Ṣeyon's salvific text into a linguistic exemplar.[311]

The *mämher* reappears in Ludolf's *Historia Aethiopica* (1681), a wide-ranging study with a chapter on Ge'ez literature. In it, Ludolf surveyed the

---

[309] Bausi and Sokolinski, *Dillmann's Lexicon*, 55.   [310] Haberland, "Ludolf," 3.
[311] See also its entries on Täsfa Ṣeyon: Ludolf, *Lexicon*, 188; cf. 194, 59; and additionally, the shorter entry in the original 1661 edition, 152.

Figure 22 *abba* Gorgoryos (nd–1658) in Hiob Ludolf, *Iobi Ludolfi Ad Suam Historiam Aethiopicam Antehac Editam Commentarius* (Frankfurt am Main: Zunner, 1691) (photo by the author)

Ethiopian Bible, and he began his treatment of the New Testament with a discussion of Täsfa Ṣeyon, a review of the distinctions between the *Testamentum Novum* and the conventional Ethiopian order of the scriptures, and Latin translations of several of Täsfa Ṣeyon's Ge'ez commentaries.[312] The first major European study of the Ethiopian scriptures, a topic that had preoccupied Latin orientalists since the sixteenth century, now rested upon Täsfa Ṣeyon's edition. Ludolf's *Lexicon* and *Historia* remained standard references for the next two centuries, notably underpinning the Ethiopia-related writing of Samuel Johnson (1709–84), Edward Gibbon (1737–94), and Denis Diderot (1713–84).[313] In 1800, the renowned French linguist Antoine Isaac Silvestre de Sacy (1758–1838), widely considered the progenitor of philological and language-focused disciplinary orientalism, used Ludolf's Ge'ez works to issue the first published translation of Enoch (Figure 23).[314]

---

[312] Ludolf, *Historia*, Vol 3, 4; cf. Vol. 3, 3, and Vol. I, 3.
[313] *EA*, Vol. 3, 299–301; Gibbon, *Decline and Fall*; Diderot and d'Alembert, *Encyclopédie*.
[314] Dehérain, *de Sacy*, 57–58; Erho and Stuckenbruck, "Ethiopic Enoch"; de Sacy, "Enoch"; Said, *Orientalism*, 123–48.

Figure 23 Silvestre de Sacy (1758–1838) (public domain)

Ludolf's religious politics were complex. In the *Historia*, he informed readers that he wrote to serve the "Christian and literary republic" as well as "the ancient nation of the Abyssinians," whose conflict with the Portuguese Jesuits had produced suspicion of all Western Christians. He further lamented that the Catholic–Protestant schism had hampered Western relations with the Eastern Christians, to say nothing of the broader struggle against the "idolatrous heathens" that surrounded them in the Muslim world.[315] This ecumenism, however, had limits. Ludolf elsewhere castigated his erstwhile assistant Johann Michael Wansleben (1635–79) when the latter converted to Catholicism and disputed his mentor's claims about the similarities of Protestant and Ethiopian Christianity,[316] and he would have surely rejected Täsfa Ṣeyon's careful elision of the differences between Ethiopian Orthodox and Catholic doctrine.[317] These confessional politics paralleled Ludolf's textual critique of Täsfa Ṣeyon's magnum opus, delivered via Gorgoryos's unflattering remarks about the printing errors in the *Testamentum Novum*.[318]

Two centuries later, Täsfa Ṣeyon was further integrated into the sinews of the orientalist academy by August Dillmann (1823–94) (Figure 24). A theologian, linguist, and philologist trained by Heinrich Fleischer (1801–88), himself a student of de Sacy, Dillmann was a prolific Ethiopian Bible scholar who is today considered a founder of Ge'ez philology.[319] This reputation principally

---

[315] Ludolf, *Historia*, unpaginated preface. [316] Hamilton, *Copts and the West*, 157.
[317] *Modus baptizandi*, IIv. [318] Ludolf, *Commentarius*, 297. [319] *EA*, Vol. 2, 61–62.

Figure 24 August Dillmann (1823–1894) (public domain)

derives from his Old Testament editions and translations – including Enoch – as well as his Ge'ez–Latin *Lexicon linguae aethiopicae* (1865), which replaced Ludolf's dictionary as the standard reference of its kind. In its introduction, Dillmann informed readers that the scriptures were peerless for the study of Ge'ez,[320] and then explained that with respect to the New Testament, he had reluctantly used Täsfa Ṣeyon's error-strewn *editio princeps* instead of an alternative base manuscript or the 1826 printed Ge'ez Gospels.[321] This decision intertwined his *Lexicon* with the *Testamentum Novum* through extensive scriptural citations and comparisons with their Greek, Latin, Hebrew, and Syriac counterparts. Täsfa Ṣeyon's text thereby entered the analytic apparatus of Semitic studies.

The intellectual gulf between Ludolf and Dillmann reflects the emerging contours of modern academic orientalism, and especially its German variant. With respect to Ethiopianist scholarship, Dillmann brokered a shift away from the early modern traditions of *philologia sacra* and world history continued by Ludolf, and toward a self-consciously positivist *philologia orientalis* predicated on lexicography, grammar, and comparative linguistics. If this new language-focused field derived much from the post-Enlightenment model of

---

[320] Dillmann, *Lexicon*, 1.   [321] Zuurmond, *Novum Testamentum*, Vol. 1, 226–34.

textual systematization exemplified by de Sacy, it also remained concerned with deepening Christian understanding. Its cultural politics, however, were new. Like many of his contemporaries, Dillmann advanced the project of intellectualizing non-Western racial inferiority.[322] In the Ethiopian context, Ge'ez literature became at once an object of scientific inquiry, an avenue to Christian truth, and an index of African deficiency. This historicist congeries explains how Dillmann could defend the Semitic richness of ancient Ge'ez and its early speakers while castigating Ethiopian apocrypha as "fictitious," Ethiopian scholars as prone to "hallucinations and conjectures," their faith as "degenerated," and their society as mired in "barbarism and darkness."[323] He judged the *liqawent* incapable of understanding their own linguistic heritage, exemplifying the confidence of mid-nineteenth-century German orientalists that the scientific quality of their analysis made them supreme arbiters of non-Western truth.[324] In the process, the study of Ethiopia itself – as distinct from its languages and texts – receded as a worthy intellectual concern, becoming reduced instead to a bounded domain of world literature.[325] These epistemic politics underpin Dillmann's critiques of Täsfa Ṣeyon's editorial deficiency, suggesting an antagonistic vision of the relationship between academic orientalism and culturally situated traditionalist scholarship. In this, the German personified the "tyranny of philology."[326]

Imagining Diaspora

This orientalist canonization anticipated Täsfa Ṣeyon's rediscovery by Ethiopian intellectuals. In 1924, Crown Prince Täfäri Mäkonnen (1892–1975) – the future Emperor Ḫaylä Śellasé – embarked on a momentous European tour. As the first overseas mission of a de facto sovereign, the tour was a milestone in Ethiopian statecraft: it instantiated a new foreign policy predicated on sustained diplomatic engagement and economic partnership with Europe, building upon Ethiopia's 1923 admission to the League of Nations.[327] That April, Täfäri Mäkonnen and a retinue of Ethiopian notables departed from Djibouti for British Mandate Palestine, where they toured the sites of the Holy Land, visited the Ethiopian monastery in Jerusalem, and celebrated Easter with its *rayes* and resident monks.[328] They then proceeded to Europe, where they visited its capitals to press acclaim. In June, they reached Rome for direct talks with fascist Prime

---
[322] Kontje, *German Orientalisms*.
[323] Dillmann, *Lexicon*, 1, 6; Dillmann and Bezold, *Ethiopic Grammar,* 12.
[324] Kontje, *German Orientalisms*, 138–39; Marchand, *Orientalism*, 83–86.
[325] Mufti, *Forget English!*   [326] El-Ariss, "Cooks and Crooks," 18.
[327] Asfa-Wossen Asserate, *King of Kings*, 52–61; De Lorenzi, *Guardians*, 94–113.
[328] Ḥeruy Wäldä Śellasé, ደስታና ክብር, 13–15.

Minister Benito Mussolini (1883–1945).[329] It would prove the only face-to-face meeting between the two leaders.

The visit produced an extraordinary historical recuperation. After a series of ominous military demonstrations, a diplomatic summit at the Palazzo Chigi, and an awkward tour of the Museo Coloniale, the Ethiopian delegation visited the Vatican for an audience with Pope Pius XI (1857–1939). In the retelling of Ḫeruy Wäldä Śellasé, the civil servant and budding writer who chronicled the tour, the travelers now wearied of their sightseeing, and stopped to rest in a quiet area behind Saint Peter's Basilica.[330] They discovered that their refuge was adjacent to Santo Stefano, now rechristened the Pontifical Ethiopian College but still known to Ethiopians – and now Eritreans – as Däbrä Qeddus Esṭifanos. Ḫeruy briefly related the history of this unusual *däbr* to his Amharic readers, and then explained that when Täfäri Mäkonnen and his companions entered Santo Stefano, they were greeted by its current Ethiopian and Eritrean residents. In the world of the text, a supposedly chance discovery produced a moment of profound metahistorical significance. The Crown Prince had followed the path blazed by centuries of intrepid Ethiopian pilgrims (Figure 25).

According to Ḫeruy, the delegation's diasporic hosts received them with a celebration recalling a religious feast. In its erudite and multilingual culture of praise, the meeting at Santo Stefano resembled a *liqawent* conclave in the heart of fascist Italy. As the visitors watched, the residents delivered a series of speeches and praise poems affirming the greatness of Täfäri Mäkonnen, the divine election of the Solomonid dynasty, and the ties of faith that linked the assembly to distant Ethiopia and the wider Christian ecumene (Figure 26). For an instant, the reader glimpses the intellectual world of the *däbr* as it might be represented in a vernacular chronicle. According to Ḫeruy, the Crown Prince was moved by "these children of Ethiopia overcome with love for their country," and when the reception concluded, the delegation toured the historic building. Ḫeruy showed particular interest in its sepulcher, whose Ge'ez epitaphs he copied, translated into Amharic, and published in his printed account of the European tour, fittingly titled *Dästanna kebber*, or *Happiness and Honour* (1924). Among them was the epitaph of Täsfa Ṣeyon.[331]

---

[329] Vedovato, *Accordi*, 8–11.   [330] Ḫeruy Wäldä Śellasé, ደስታና ክብር, 71–75.
[331] Ḫeruy Wäldä Selassé, ደስታና ክብር, 75.

L'ILLUSTRAZIONE ITALIANA

Anno LI. - N. 26. - 29 Giugno 1924.   Questo numero costa L. 2,60 (Est., L. 5).

RAS TAFARI, REGGENTE D'ETIOPIA, A ROMA.

Figure 25 Crown Prince Täfäri Mäkonnen visits the Vatican in 1924, *L'Illustrazione italiana*, 29 June 1924 (photo by the author)

Ḥeruy concluded his account of Santo Stefano by reflecting on the achievements of these early modern pilgrims, the devotion of the current residents, and the historical significance of an Ethiopian space at the heart of global Catholicism. "To find Ethiopian monasteries in Jerusalem and Rome is a great point of pride for all the children of Ethiopia," he remarked, "and this explains

Figure 26 Crown Prince Täfäri Mäkonnen visits Santo Stefano in 1924, Ḫeruy Wäldä Śellasé, ደስታና ክብር የኢትዮጵያ መንግሥት አልጋ ወራሽና እንደራሴ ልዑል ተፈሪ መኮንን ወደ አውሮፓ ሲሄዱና ሲመለሱ የመንገዳቸው አኳኋን (አዲስ አበባ፣ ተፈሪ መኮንን ማተሚያ ቤት፣ 1916 ዓም)

why Ethiopian Christianity has endured since many earlier times."[332] The accommodating Vatican *däbr* at the holy places in Rome seemed an epitome of Ethiopia's transcendent history, much as Pope Francis would suggest a century later. Nearly 500 years after Täsfa Ṣeyon's exile, Ḫeruy textually repatriated him through the print medium they both celebrated, transforming the *mämher* into a paragon of the Ethiopian diaspora and ecumene. This was the first notice of Täsfa Ṣeyon in Ethiopian literature.

One year later, this Amharic travelogue had a curious sequel. It was penned by André Jarosseau (1858–1941), a French Capuchin missionary who was the childhood tutor of Täfäri Mäkonnen.[333] In 1925, the Tipografia Vaticana issued his bilingual *Aċher yäbétä krestiyan katolikawit tarik*, or *Short History of the Catholic Church*, distinctive for its unusual facing pages of Amharic and Oromo text.[334] Intended for Ethiopia's growing network of Catholic mission schools, Jarosseau began his survey with ancient Israel before addressing the arrival of Christianity in Ethiopia, the development of the Solomonid monarchy, the sixteenth-century Adal-Ottoman conflict, and the concurrent development of European–Ethiopian relations – from the diplomacy of Paul III to the first Catholic patriarchs of Ethiopia. After attending to the modern era, he

---

[332] Ḫeruy Wäldä Selassé, ደስታና ክብር, 75: "በኢየሩሳሌምና በሮምያ በርምያ የኢትዮጵያ ገዳም መገኘት ለኢትዮጵያ ልጆች ሁሉ ታላቅ መመኪያ ነው። ይኸውም የኢትዮጵያ ክርስቲያንነት ከበዙ ዘመን በፊት የቆየ መሆኑን ያስረዳል።"

[333] *EA*, Vol. 3, 270. [334] *Abunä* Endreyas [Jarosseau], ታሪh.

concluded with a discussion of "the ancient Ethiopian monastery in the city of Rome." It is a uniquely synchronic and monolingual chapter, written only in Amharic. Echoing Ḥeruy, Jarosseau cast Santo Stefano as an implicit synthesis of Ethiopia's role in the encompassing universal history he had just outlined. He informed readers that the graves of Ethiopian priests and monks could be found "within an ancient church" inside the Vatican, and listed the names of Täsfa Ṣeyon and the other pilgrims buried in its sepulcher. He then described Santo Stefano's foundation and transformation into the Pontifical Ethiopian College, adding that its residents had joyously welcomed the Crown Prince on a recent visit to Rome. He concluded with another Ḥeruy-esque reflection on "Jerusalem the Holy City of David" and "Rome the Great City of Caesar," which Jarosseau judged the most enduring of God's ancient creations.[335] In a glimpse of his imagined locus of African Catholicism, he paired this discussion of Santo Stefano with a photo of Pius XI – the only image in the entire work. Stripped of their once-distinctive *täwaḥedo* Orthodox identity, Täsfa Ṣeyon and the Ethiopian *däbr* of Rome were here subsumed within the official history of the Catholic Church.

Colonizing Santo Stefano

As this development suggests, Santo Stefano was by this time a potent signifier in the Italian colonial imaginary, which flourished after the kingdom's formal subjugation of present-day Eritrea (1882), Somalia (1905), and Libya (1911). A key exponent of this connection was Carlo Conti Rossini (1872–1949), among the most distinguished Italian orientalists of the era.[336] Trained by Ignazio Guidi (1844–1935), a specialist in Eastern Christian philology and founder of Italian Semitic studies, Conti Rossini served in the liberal-era Eritrean and Libyan colonial administrations before assuming a position at the University of Rome, additionally teaching at the fascist-era Ministry of the Colonies.[337] By the 1930s, he had issued more than one hundred publications, encompassing Ethiopian history, linguistics, philology, folklore, and bibliography, and he additionally wrote nonspecialist works that purported to situate colonial affairs in their world-historical context.[338] His stature as a public intellectual and regime orientalist was such that his academic studies were acclaimed in the popular press.

---

[335] *Abunä* Endreyas [Jarosseau], ታሪh, 142: "ቅድስት እየሩሳሌም የዳዊት ከተማና ታላቂቱ ሮማ የቄሳር ከተማ ከዱር ፍጥረት ሁሉ ቆይም የቀሩት እሌህ [እነዚህ] ሁሉቱ ብቻ ናቸው።"

[336] *EA*, Vol. 1, 791–792.   [337] "Funzionari coloniali."

[338] Chakrabarty, *Provincializing Europe*; Guha, *World-History*.

If Dillmann asserted the linguistic synecdoche of Ethiopianist orientalism, Conti Rossini adapted this epistemic framework to historiography. He understood this pursuit as the application of Semiticist philological tools to Rankean source criticism, then the dominant methodology within the international historical discipline. This hybrid approach suffuses his *Storia d'Etiopia* (1928), a study of Ethiopian antiquity that secured his reputation as the preeminent Italian specialist of his generation.[339] In its introduction, he positioned himself as Dillmann's successor, and then surveyed the development of European Ethiopianist scholarship, which in his view began in sixteenth-century Italy. The Venetian presence in the Levant brought Ethiopian pilgrims to Rome, which in turn provoked a Vatican curiosity about Ethiopian Christianity, culminating in the establishment of Santo Stefano – "a modest seedbed of Ethiopian studies in Europe."

For Conti Rossini, this fecundity was exemplified by Täsfa Ṣeyon. He judged the latter an "active and educated" figure who exceeded the station of his diasporic kin to acquire "a certain fame" among the Roman elite, enhanced by his adoption of "the perhaps unauthorized title of secretary of King Gälawdéwos." Täsfa Ṣeyon, he opined, was "struck by the superiority of European civilization," which inspired his embrace of print to restore devastated Ethiopia. These sentiments inspired the *Testamentum Novum*, and additionally led him to instruct his Italian students Gualtieri and Vittori. Conti Rossini judged the last a double pioneer. If his 1552 Ge'ez grammar "prepared the path for future researchers," it was also for Conti Rossini the first instance of Ethiopian historiography, since it presented a chronology of Ethiopian rulers. For this reason, he concluded, the writing of Ethiopian history was "born in Italy," and not Ethiopia.[340]

Modern developments followed suit. In Conti Rossini's estimation, the nineteenth-century European exploration of Africa and concurrent development of Egyptology, Assyriology, and Indology fueled European interest in the scientific study of Ethiopian literature. Dillmann personified this conjuncture, and he and his successors advanced the European understanding of Ethiopia by establishing the Semitic studies subfield that included Conti Rossini's teacher Guidi. Fittingly, the latter had learned Ge'ez from the works of Ludolf and Dillmann, and Amharic from *däbtära* Keflä Giyorgis (1825–1908), an erudite fin-de-siècle resident of Santo Stefano who collaborated with Guidi on several major works.[341] Through this latter connection, Conti Rossini affirmed, Santo Stefano had "once again come to the service of science."[342] The encompassing

---

[339] Conti Rossini, *Storia d'Etiopia*. [340] Conti Rossini, *Storia d'Etiopia*, 12.
[341] *EA*, Vol. 3, 370–71. [342] Conti Rossini, *Storia d'Etiopia*, 28.

intellectual genealogy of his teacher thus framed his own study as the culmination of a distinctive Italian orientalist lineage originating at Santo Stefano. Reviews of his book even mentioned this connection, highlighting Täsfa Ṣeyon's contribution to the Italian nationalist project of knowing and subjugating Ethiopia.[343]

These arguments were soon weaponized. In 1934, Ethiopian and Italian troops clashed at a remote outpost on the Somali frontier, triggering a ten-month international crisis. As the world followed the diplomatic drama at the League, Italian specialists rallied themselves to the intellectual task of undermining Ethiopian sovereignty, offering academic studies of Ethiopian backwardness and failed statehood, on the one hand, and the historic longevity and beneficence of Italian involvement in the Horn, on the other. If the first position was exemplified by Conti Rossini, the second was typified by the Roman archivist, historian, and journalist Renato Lefevre (1909–2004), who reconstructed Italy's late medieval contacts with the Horn and the corresponding early modern European imagination of Ethiopia.[344] This historiographic legitimation of the colonial project ascribed a new significance to Santo Stefano.

The most prominent commentary on this theme came from Mario Pigli, a fascist journalist and party official who was in the 1930s the chief editor of *L'Azione coloniale*, the official propaganda weekly of the Istituto Coloniale Fascista.[345] His *La civiltà italiana e l'Etiopia* (1935), published under the bizarre pseudonym "Gihâd" ("Jihad"), popularized Italian academic research on Mediterraneanism and premodern Italo-Ethiopian contacts, suggesting that Italy was an eternal protector of Ethiopia. A key development in this history was the emergence of the Ethiopian community at Santo Stefano, which Pigli erratically surveyed in a chapter entitled "Italy Makes a Home for Her African Children." Among its protagonists was Täsfa Ṣeyon, now a paragon of "Roman generosity." Stripping the *mämher* from his historical context, Pigli reimagined him as a proof of perennial Italo-Ethiopian fraternity, personifying Italy's commitment to its long-frustrated civilizing mission in Ethiopia, now poised to resume via the imminent colonial invasion.[346] The international English language editions of Pigli's book were among the most widely read works of Italian propaganda during the Italo-Ethiopian crisis. Through them, Täsfa Ṣeyon was now cast in the international drama of empire.

---

[343] "Lo storiografo dell'Etiopia." [344] Lefevre, "Prete Gianni"; Lefevre, *Terra nostra*.
[345] Deplano, *Africa in casa*, 80–81. [346] Gihâd [Pigli], *Civiltà italiana*, 55.

Imperial Refuge

On October 3, 1935, Emilio De Bono (1866–1944) ordered his troops across the Ethiopian frontier. The following May, Mussolini announced the establishment of the new colony of Africa Orientale Italiana, comprised of Eritrea, Somalia, and the now-subjugated Ethiopia. But the imagined eternal fascist empire proved fleeting. Over the next five years, the colony remained in a constant state of insurrection and counterinsurgency, even as the colonial administration attempted to co-opt the Ethiopian elite and engineer a cohort of African colonial functionaries. A cultural ancillary of these developments was the transformation of Santo Stefano into a symbol of the Italo-Ethiopian colonial relationship, fruitful "native" collaboration, and African sanctuary.

Glimpses of this shift appear in the writing of Ethiopian detainees and exiles. In 1937, the regime extended its system of extrajudicial remote confinement to its African colonial subjects, under the direction of the Ministry of Italian Africa. The latter's coordinating Office of Political Affairs was then led by the orientalist and colonial official Enrico Cerulli (1898–1988), who selected Tivoli as the carceral site for Ethiopian detainees he deemed susceptible to political cooptation.[347] The symbolism is striking, in that Tivoli was the final home of Täsfa Ṣeyon, now an avatar of Italo-Ethiopian harmony. If Cerulli appreciated this history,[348] it was also grasped by some of the detainees. Among them was a Catholic civil servant named Berhanä Marqos Wäldä Ṣadiq (1892–1943), who spent months in Tivoli negotiating his freedom with Cerulli.[349] Recalling this difficult time, his family remembers that Berhanä Marqos reflected on his childhood reading of Jarosseau's Amharic history of Catholicism and the parallels between his displacement and the exiled Täsfa Ṣeyon.[350] The image of the uprooted *mämher* comforted Berhanä Marqos amid the dislocation, material hardship, and routinized violence of colonial rule. The Roman *däbr* was once again a diasporic refuge.

Other detainees sought to mobilize this history. During this same period, Santo Stefano was invoked by Ethiopian prisoners at Asinara, a desolate island north of Sardinia that had become the largest African penal colony in the Italian metropole. Between 1937 and 1940, it maintained hundreds of Ethiopian and Eritrean detainees whom Cerulli had identified as neither

---

[347] Notes for Enrico Cerulli, dated July 27, 1937, ASMAI, pos. 181/54.
[348] Cerulli, "Documenti."
[349] Berhanä Marqos to Enrico Cerulli, Nähase 17, 1929 AM, Tivoli, ASMAI, pos. 181/54.
[350] Mickael Bethe-Sélassié, *Jeune Éthiopie*, 136–37.

useful nor dangerous. They were stranded, and with little to offer the regime in a bargain of collaboration, they could only petition for freedom. In 1937, a civil servant named Asfaw Andargé wrote Cerulli, introducing himself as a devoted Catholic and wrongfully detained supporter of Italy. He requested relocation to the Pontifical Ethiopian College, where he would be able to continue his "spiritual studies" and learn "a bit of Italian," so as to better serve the regime.[351] Around this same time, a group of Orthodox ecclesiastics also dispatched a letter from Asinara to Minister of the Colonies Alessandro Lessona (1891–1991), Cerulli's superior and Mussolini's immediate subordinate (Figure 27). They introduced themselves as loyal servants of the church who had pacified the Ethiopian faithful after the Italian invasion. One of them, *liqä liqawent* Gäbrä'ab Mängestu, had in fact shocked Addis Ababa residents by publicly blessing the colonial state.[352] Given these politics, the group requested permission to visit "the tombs of Saint Peter and Saint Paul, the leaders of the apostles who founded our church."[353] Several years later, the spirit of these requests was honored by *abba* Pétros Haylu, the erudite prefect of the Pontifical Ethiopian College, who used his office to advocate on behalf of an Eritrean arrested in Bologna (Figure 28).[354] Meanwhile, seminarian and College alumnus *abba* Gäbräyäsus Haylu (1906–93) secretly penned a Tigrinya novel about the debasing brutality of Italian colonial rule.[355] These acts suggest the Ethiopian detainees were right to seek refuge at Santo Stefano. It also explains the regime's surveillance of the College as a metropolitan space uniquely reserved for African colonial subjects.[356]

Meanwhile, Haylä Sellasé was exiled in Bath. He spent his days lobbying the League and coordinating the resistance in Ethiopia, and at night, he wrote his memoirs with Heruy Wäldä Sellasé, now his Foreign Minister and closest advisor. Heruy had become the most prominent Ethiopian diplomat and intellectual of his generation, and his years of travel, government experience, and personal service to the emperor ideally qualified him for the task of

---

[351] Amharic letter from Asfaw Andargé to Enrico Cerulli, dated 29 Säné 1929AM, ASMAI pos. 181/54.
[352] Bälätä Gäbré, የጉዞ ትዝታ, 99.
[353] Amharic letter from Ethiopian detainees to Minister of the Colonies, undated, ASMAI, pos. 181/54: "የኔታችን መሠረተ ቤተ ክርስቲያን የሊቀ ሐዋርያትን የቅዱስ ጴጥሮስና የቅዱስ ጳውሎስን መቃብር"
[354] Letter from Minister of Italian Africa to Ministry of the Interior, dated 11 May, 1945, ASMAI AP cart. 83/245.
[355] Gäbräyäsus Haylu, ሓደ ዛንታ, unpaginated preface; *EA*, Vol. 2, 630–31.
[356] See ACS, Ministero dell'Africa Italiana, Affari Politici Archivio Segreto, bust. 24.

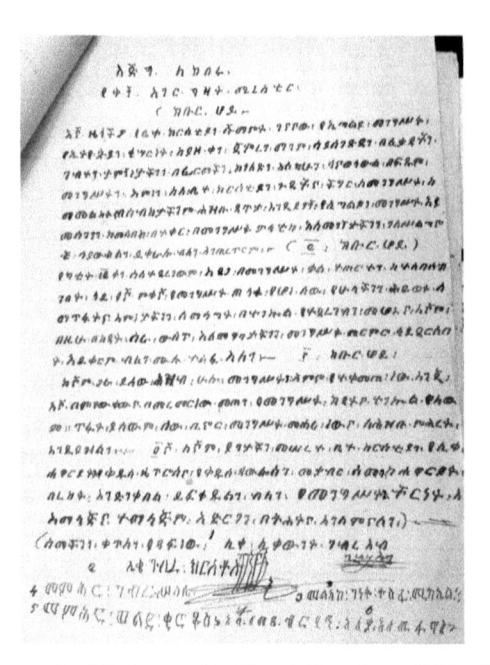

Figure 27 Letter to the Minister of Italian Africa from Ethiopians detained at Asinara, ASMAI AP cart. 83/245 (photo by the author)

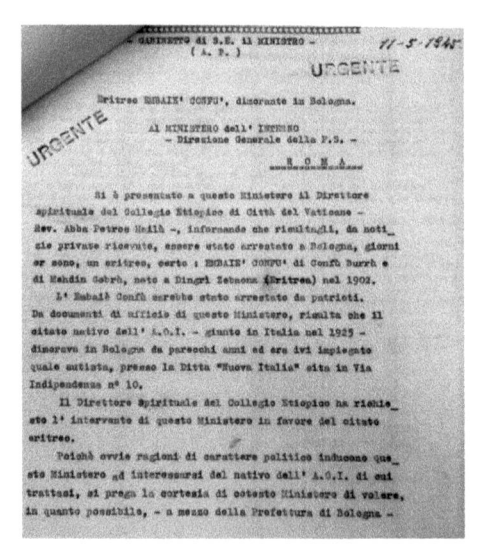

Figure 28 Telegram from the Ministry of the Colonies to the Ministry of the Interior, 1945, ASMAI pos. 181/54 (photo by the author)

official biography. Reminiscing in Bath about their 1924 tour of Europe, Ḥeruy observed that if the Italians of the present were to remember the visit, they would be shocked by the warm reception the Ethiopians had once received from the Roman masses.[357] Täsfa Ṣeyon and Santo Stefano, however, were now fraught topics, and Ḥeruy minimized the role of the Italian *däbr* in the memoirs. With respect to the 1924 tour, his new narrative focused on the official Italian reception and duplicitous treaty negotiations at the Palazzo Chigi, while the delegation's reception at Santo Stefano, which consumes half of the Italian chapter in Ḥeruy's 1924 travelogue, was curtailed to two short paragraphs in the wartime memoirs.[358] Täsfa Ṣeyon's name was also excised from the text. The hardship of exile and unfolding colonial violence in Ethiopia had diminished the metahistorical significance Ḥeruy once ascribed to the *mämher* and his diasporic kin. This violence had been specifically directed at Däbrä Libanos, Täsfa Ṣeyon's alma mater. The 1937 mass killing at the monastery is today remembered as among the most horrific Italian crimes of the colonial era.

Renaissance Past, Postcolonial Future

By 1941, Africa Orientale Italiana had collapsed. Amid the drama of decolonization and the postwar settlement, some Italian and Ethiopian intellectuals used the legacy of Santo Stefano to reimagine the future of European–African relations and the reconciliation of colonizer and colonized. Paradoxically, this metaphor was forcefully espoused by Cerulli, now an ex-colonial official and accused war criminal.[359] In the 1950s, he repeatedly suggested that Ethiopians and Italians should look to the "secular" sixteenth-century model of Santo Stefano to transcend the warped mentalities of colonialism, as these were then being theorized by philosophers like Léopold Sédar Senghor (1906–2001) and Albert Memmi (1920–2020).[360] Other Italian intellectuals offered similar platitudes to the Pan-African activists gathered at the 1959 Congress of Negro Writers and Artists in Rome.[361] These interventions jointly suggested that the postcolonial future should revive an ostensibly apolitical precolonial past, now caricatured through the extra-imperial heuristic of Renaissance Mediterraneanism. This liberal humanist appeal effaced the recent trauma of colonial rule and elided the active question of postcolonial justice, complementing similarly exonerative tendencies in Cerulli's own scholarship.

---

[357] Haylä Śellasé [with Ḥeruy Wäldä Śellasé], ሕይወቴና የኢትዮጵያ እርምጃ, 76.
[358] Haylä Śellasé [with Ḥeruy Wäldä Śellasé], ሕይወቴና የኢትዮጵያ እርምጃ, 80; cf. Ḥeruy Wäldä Śellasé, ደስታና ክብር, 71–75.
[359] De Lorenzi, "Orientalist on Trial."   [360] Cerulli, "Nuovo posto."
[361] Dorato, "[Discours d'accueil]."

Meanwhile, Ethiopian and Eritrean intellectuals began to link Santo Stefano to Ethiopia's stormy relationship with the wider world. Some Eritrean Catholics, for example, viewed Täsfa Ṣeyon as a progenitor of African Catholicism, most notably Täklä Maryam Sämharay Sälim (1871–1942), who used Täsfa Ṣeyon's works to defend the Catholic Ge'ez liturgy.[362] Other intellectuals reimagined Santo Stefano in the context of the prevailing historical narrative of an enduring "Greater Ethiopia." In the mid-1960s, the historian Täklä Ṣadeq Mäkwuriya (1913–2000) discussed the monastery in his account of the reign of Gälawdéwos, which he understood within the conjuncture of the Ottoman–Portuguese imperial contest and the Catholic missionary enterprise in Ethiopia.[363] Some years later, on the eve of the 1974 revolution, historian Alämé Eshäté (nd–2011) began his study of Ethiopian diasporic history with Täsfa Ṣeyon, who he suggested inaugurated an outward-looking educational quest that stretched from the early modern era through the student movements of the 1960s.[364] If the orientalists had reduced Täsfa Ṣeyon to an instrument of exogenous linguistic understanding or an exemplar of ennobling European tutelage, these Ethiopian and Eritrean intellectuals instead joined Ḥeruy in imagining the *mämher* as a synecdoche of Ethiopia's encounter with the West.

For the contemporary Catholic Church, meanwhile, Täsfa Ṣeyon came to exemplify the transformative globalizing ethos of Vatican II and the vibrant history of African Catholicism. If these concerns underpinned Pope Francis's 2020 speech at the Pontifical Ethiopian College, they were perhaps first espoused by *abba* Samuel Asghedom (1915–nd), an alumnus of the Eritrean mission schools and Pontifical Gregorian University in Rome. After a distinguished career as an ecclesiastic, writer, and journalist, he became rector of the Pontifical Ethiopian College amid the intellectual foment of Vatican II, its debates about internationalizing the Church, and the 1960 elevation of the first African cardinal, Laurean Rugambwa (1912–97) of Tanzania.[365] In 1972, he attended the Fourth International Conference of Ethiopian Studies, convened in Rome by Cerulli, where he boldly argued that Täsfa Ṣeyon and his Italian collaborators offered a model of dialogic intercultural scholarship that could instruct contemporary academics. This point, in his view, was exemplified by

---

[362] Täklä Maryam Sämḥaray Sälim, *Messe éthiopienne*, 2.
[363] Täklä Ṣadeq Mäkwuriya, የኢትዮጵያ ታሪህ, 59–60. See also IES Ms. 327, an Amharic history by Gäbrä Mika'él Germu (1900–69) that discusses Ethiopian-European relations and the Jesuit missions.
[364] Alämé Eshäté, "የተማሩ ኢትዮጵያውያች ታሪህ," 115–16.
[365] Foster, *African Catholic*, 257; Puglisi, *Chi è?*, 267.

the *Testamentum Novum*: if the text was "a revelation for the world of the [European] savants," it was also true that its crisp fidäl and portable material form were "more suited to the needs of the Ethiopian pilgrims than the culture of [European] researchers."[366] Its worldliness and multiple readerships was the point. Moreover, *abba* Samuel added that Täsfa Ṣeyon's student Gualtieri always honored his teacher in his own publications, a mutual respect maintained by their modern successors Käflä Giyorgis and Guidi, the latter being "the last

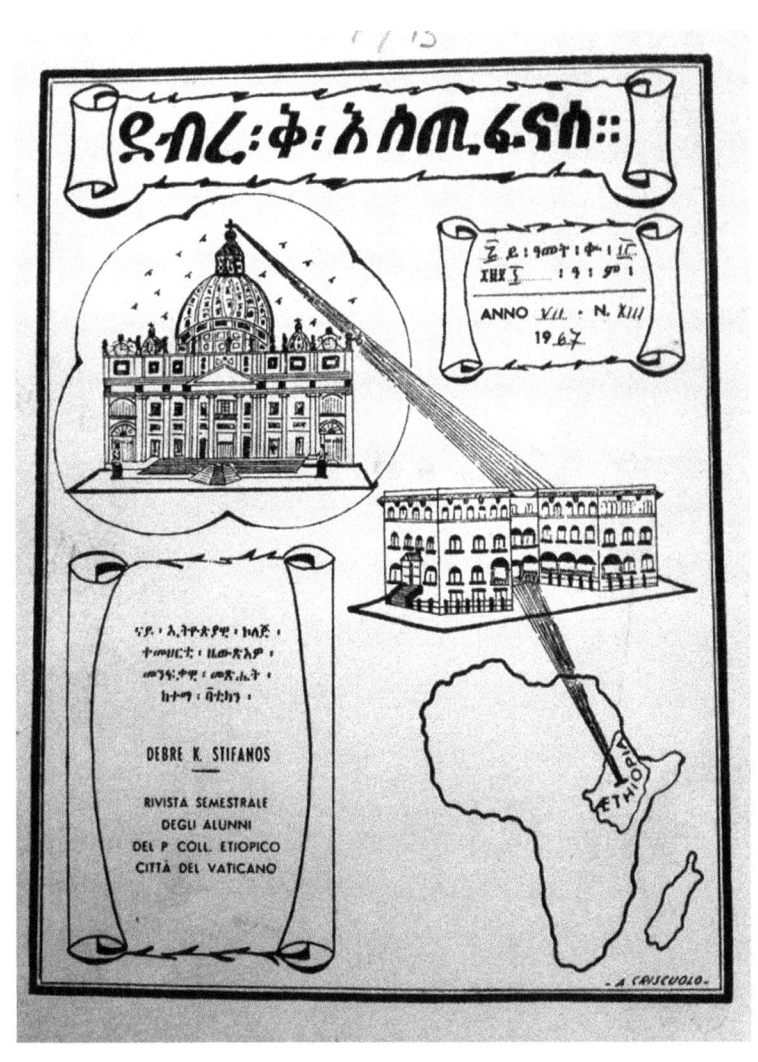

Figure 29 Cover, ደብረ ቅ[ዱስ] እስጢፋኖስ 7, no. 13 (1967) (photo by the author)

---
[366] Samuel Asghedom, "Santo Stefano," 398–99.

disciple" of the *däbr*. Read closely, *abba* Samuel's words suggest that the epistemic antagonism between academic philology and situated traditionalist knowledge posited by orientalists like Dillmann was intellectually impoverishing, better abandoned for the dynamic of equitable intellectual partnership represented by the Santo Stefano tradition of knowledge production. If the spirit of this position was not especially evident in the specialist academic field, it was preserved in the pages of the College's multilingual and interdisciplinary publication *Däbrä q[eddus] esṭifanos*, which regularly featured articles on Täsfa Ṣeyon, Ethiopian Christianity, and the history of Catholic-Eastern Christian dialogue (Figure 29). Cerulli was among its benefactors.[367] It is a telling connection. In a world marked by division and the scars of the past, including those inflicted or condoned by the colonial state, the institutional church, and the modern academy, the realized *accoglienza* of Santo Stefano suggested a path toward authentic reconciliation and intellectual cosmopolitanism.

---

[367] Raineri, *Inventario*, 277; "Conferenze."

Glossary
(Amharic, Tigrinya, and Ge'ez, unless otherwise stated)

abba   Religious honorific, lit. "Father."

abun(ä)   Metropolitan of the Ethiopian Orthodox Church; monastic father

aqqabé sä'at   Keeper of the hours; abbot of Däbrä Hayq, royal counsellor

condottiere   Professional military leader (Italian)

däbr   Monastery

däbtära   Unordained clergy, cantor

dhimmī   Christian and Jewish minorities in Muslim societies (Arabic)

eçhägé   Abbot of Däbrä Libanos and administrative head of the Ethiopian Orthodox Church

familia papae   Papal family or household (Latin)

fidäl   Script used for Ge'ez, Amharic, Tigrinya, and other Ethiopian and Eritrean languages

gädam   Remote monastery

gäṭär   Rural parish

kätäma   Royal court, later city

liq/liqawent   Church scholar(s)

liqä diyaqonat   Head of the deacons

liqä kahenat   Archpriest

liqä liqawent   "Head of the Scholars"

mäggabi   Administrator

mämher   Teacher, also a monastic title

natio/nationes   Foreign or minority communities of Rome (Latin)

neguś   King

philologia sacra   Scholarly study of sacred texts (Latin) *qāḍī* Judge or specialist in Islamic law (Arabic)

qomos High priest

rayes Monastic title of authority

ṣähafé te'ezaz Court historian

tabot Tablet ark

täwaḥedo Miaphysite Orthodox

Bibliography

I Archival Sources

Archivio Apostolico Vaticano [AAV], Vatican City
Archivio Centrale dello Stato [ACS], Rome
Archivio di Stato di Firenze [ASF], Florence
Archivio di Stato di Roma [ASR], Rome
Archivio Storico del Ministero dell'Africa Italiana [ASMAI], Rome
Archivio Storico del Ministero dell'Africa Italiana, Affari Politici [ASMAI AP], Rome
Biblioteca Apostolica Vaticana [BAV], Vatican City
Biblioteca Comunale di Palermo [BCP], Palermo
Biblioteca degli Intronati [BI], Siena
Biblioteca Nazionale Centrale di Firenze [BNCF], Firenze
British Library [BL], London
Institute of Ethiopian Studies [IES], Addis Ababa

II Published Sources: Ethiopian and Eritrean Languages

Alämé Eshäté. "በቀድሞ ዘመናት ከ 1889 ዓ. ም. በፊት ውጭ አገር የተማሩ ኢትዮጵያውያኖች ታሪክ።"*Ethiopian Journal of Education* 6, no. 1 (1973): 115–48.

Bäläṭä Gäbré. የጉዞ ትዝታ። አዲስ አበባ፣ ቼምበር ማተሚያ ቤት፣ 2004 ዓም።

Endreyas, *abunä* [André Jarosseau]. *Raga gababa kan ekklezia katholika*. አጭር የቤተ ክርስቲያንካቶሊካዊት ታሪክ። ሮማ፣ ባቲካን መሐተምያ፣ 1917 ዓም።

Gäbräyäsus Ḥaylu. ሐደ ዛንታ። አሥመራ፣ ቤት ማኅተም ጼጥሮስ ሲላ፣ 1942 ዓም።

Ḥeruy Wäldä Śelassé. ደስታ ክብር የኢትዮያ መንግሥት አልጋ ወራሽ እንደራሴ ልዑል ተፈሪ መኮንን ወደ አውሮፓ ሲሄዱና ሲመለሱ የመንገዳቸው አኳኋን። አዲስ አበባ፣ ተፈሪ መኮንን ማተሚያ ቤት፣ 1916 ዓም።

— . ዋዜማ። በማግሥቱ የኢትዮጵያን ነገሥታት የታሪክ በዓል ለማክበር። አዲስ አበባ፣ ጎሐ ጽባሕ፣ 1921 ዓም።

— . መጽሐፈ ቅኔ፣ ዘቀደምት ወደኃርት ሊቃውንቲሃ ወማዕምራኒሃ ለኢትዮጵያ። አዲስ አበባ፣ 1918 ዓም።

Ḥaylä Śellasé [with Ḥeruy Wäldä Śellasé]. ሕይወቴና የኢትዮጵያ አርምጃ። አዲስ አበባ፣ ብርሃንና ሰላም ማተሚያ ቤት፣ 1965 ዓም።

Täklä Ṣadeq Mäkwuriya. የኢትዮጵያ ታሪክ። ከዐፄ ልብነ ድንግል እስከ ዐፄ ቴዎድሮስ። አዲስ አበባ፣ አርቲስቲክ ማተሚያ ቤት፣ 1945 ዓም።

III Published Sources: European and Other Languages

Adankpo-Labadie, Olivia. "A Faith between Two Worlds: Expressing Ethiopian Devotion and Crossing Cultural Boundaries at Santo Stefano dei Mori in Early Modern Rome." In *A Companion to Religious Minorities in Early Modern Rome*, edited by Emily Michelson and Matthew Coneys Wainwright, 169–91. Leiden: Brill, 2021.

― *Moines, saints et hérétiques dans l'Éthiopie médiévale*. Rome: École française, 2023.

Alden, Dauril. *The Making of an Enterprise: The Society of Jesus in Portugal, Its Empire, and beyond, 1540–1750*. Stanford: Stanford University Press, 1996.

Ali, Omar H. *Malik Ambar: Power and Slavery across the Indian Ocean*. New York: Oxford University Press, 2016.

Ališan, Łewond. Հայապատում. Venice: 1901.

Álvares, Francisco. *La Historia d'Ethiopia di Francesco Alvarez*. Edited by Ludovico Beccadelli and Osvaldo Raineri. Vatican City: Biblioteca Apostolica Vaticana, 2007.

― *Ho Preste Ioam das Indias: verdadera informaçam das terras do Preste Ioam*. Lisbon: L. Rodrigues, 1540.

App, Urs. *The Birth of Orientalism*. Philadelphia: University of Pennsylvania Press, 2011.

Asfa-Wossen Asserate. *King of Kings: The Triumph and Tragedy of Emperor Haile Selassie I of Ethiopia*. London: Haus, 2015.

Aubin, Jean. "Le Prêtre Jean devant la censure portugaise." *Bulletin des études portugaises et brésiliennes* 41 (1980): 33–57.

Baghdiantz-McCabe, Ina. *Orientalism in Early Modern France: Eurasian Trade, Exoticism, and the Ancien Régime*. New York: Berg, 2008.

Bandini, Giovanna. "Notizie sugli artigiani ceramisti a Roma tra quattrocento e cinquecento." In *L'antica Basilica di San Lorenzo in Damaso*, edited by Cristoph Luitpold Frommel, Massimo Pentiricci, and Johannes Georg Deckers, Vol. 1, 497–505. Rome: De Luca, 2009.

Barberi, Francesco. "Libri e stampatori nella Roma dei papi." *Studi romani* 13, no. 4 (1965): 433–56.

Bardakjian, Kevork B. "The Rise of the Armenian Patriarchate of Constantinople." In *Christians and Jews in the Ottoman Empire: The Functioning of a Plural Society*, edited by Benjamin Braude and Bernard Lewis, 87–98. New York: Holmes and Meier, 1982.

Bausi, Alessandro, and Eugenia Sokolinski, eds. *150 Years after Dillmann's Lexicon: Perspectives and Challenges of Gəʽəz Studies*. Wiesbaden: Harrassowitz, 2016.

Bausi, Alessandro, and Jacopo Gnisci. "'Medieval' Ethiopia." In *Oxford Research Encyclopedia of African History*. 2024. https://doi.org/10.1093/acrefore/9780190277734.013.1082.

Beccari, Camillo. *Rerum aethiopicarum scriptores occidentales inediti a saeculo XVI ad XIX*. Rome: C. De Luigi, 1903–1917.

Beckingham, Charles Fraser, and Bernard Hamilton, eds. *Prester John, the Mongols, and the Ten Lost Tribes*. Aldershot: Ashgate Variorum, 1996.

Bernardi Salvetti, Caterina. *S. Maria degli Angeli alle Terme e Antonio Lo Duca*. Rome: Desclée, 1965.

Bernardinello, Silvio. *Autografi greci e greco-latini in occidente*. Padua: CEDAM, 1979.

Brusciotto, Giacinto. *Regulæ quædam pro difficillimi congensium idiomatis faciliori captu ad grammaticæ normam redactæ*. Rome: Typis S. Congr. de Prop. Fide, 1659.

Busi, Giulio, and Raphael Ebgi. *Giovanni Pico della Mirandola. Mito, magia, Qabbalah*. Turin: Einaudi, 2014.

Cardinali, Giacomo. *Il Cardinale Maraviglioso: l'avventura editoriale di Marcello Cervini (1539–1555)*. Geneva: Droz, 2022.

——— "Ritratto di Marcello Cervini en orientaliste. Prima parte." *Bibliothèque d'Humanisme et Renaissance* LXXX, no. 1 (2018): 77–98.

Casale, Giancarlo. *The Ottoman Age of Exploration*. Oxford: Oxford University Press, 2010.

Cerulli, Enrico. *Etiopi in Palestina: Storia della comunità etiopica di Gerusalemme*. 2 Volumes. Rome: Libreria dello Stato, 1943–1947.

——— "Il nuovo posto dell'Italia nel continente africano." *Africa* 14, no. 4 (1959): 175–76.

——— "L'Etiopia del secolo XV in nuovi documenti storici." *Africa italiana* 5 (1933): 80–99.

Chaîne, Marius. "Un monastère éthiopien a Rome aux XV et XVI siècle, Santo Stefano dei Mori." *Mélanges de la faculté orientale* V (1911): 1–36.

Chakrabarty, Dipesh. *Provincializing Europe: Postcolonial Thought and Historical Difference*. Princeton: Princeton University Press, 2000.

Clossey, Luke. *Salvation and Globalization in the Early Jesuit Missions*. New York: Cambridge University Press, 2008.

"Come si formano i funzionari coloniali." *Italia coloniale* 6, no. 7 (1929): 126–27.

Coneys Wainwright, Matthew, and Emily Michelson. "Introduction." In *A Companion to Religious Minorities in Early Modern Rome*, edited by

Matthew Coneys Wainwright and Emily Michelson, 1–12. Leiden: Brill, 2021.

"Conferenze di S.E. Prof. E. Cerulli sulla Let[t]eratura dell'Ethiopia [sic] cristiana ed il suo valore." ደብረ ቅ[ዱ]ስ አስጢፋኖስ 4, no. 2 (1965): 22–34.

Conti Rossini, Carlo. "L'autobiografia di Pāwlos monaco abissino del secolo XVI." *Rendiconti della Reale Accademia dei Lincei. Classe di scienze morali, storiche e filologiche* 5, no. 27 (1913): 279–96.

———. *Storia d'Etiopia*. Bergamo: Istituto italiano d'arti grafiche, 1928.

Contini, Riccardo. "I primordi della linguistica semitica comparata nell'Europa rinascimentale: le institutiones di Angelo Canini (1554)." *Annali di Ca' Foscari* 33, no. 3 (1994): 39–56.

Corsali, Andrea. *Lettera di Andrea Corsali all'Illustrissimo Signore Duca Iuliano de Medici. Venuta dell'India del Mese di Octobre Nel M.D.XVI.* Florence: Stephano di Carlo da Pavia, 1516.

———. *Lettera di Andrea Corsali allo ill. principe et signore Laurentio de Medici duca d'Urbino. Ex India. MDXII.* Florence: 1518.

Crawford, Osbert Guy Stanhope, ed. *Ethiopian Itineraries, circa 1400–1524.* Cambridge: Hakluyt Society, 1958.

Crummey, Donald. "Ethiopia in the Early Modern Period: Solomonic Monarchy and Christianity." *Journal of Early Modern History* 8, no. 3/4 (2004): 191–209.

Daniel Assefa. "The Archangel Uriel in 1 Enoch and Other Ethiopian Texts." In *Rediscovering Enoch? The Antediluvian Past from the Fifteenth to Nineteenth Centuries*, edited by Ariel Hessayon, Annette Yoshiko Reed, and Gabriele Boccaccini, 326–55. Leiden: Brill, 2023.

Daniels III, David D., and Lawrence Anglin. "Luther and the Ethiopian Deacon." *Lutheran Quarterly* 32, no. 4 (2018): 428–34.

De Lorenzi, James. *Guardians of the Tradition: Historians and Historical Writing in Ethiopia and Eritrea*. Rochester: University of Rochester Press, 2015.

———. "The Orientalist on Trial: Enrico Cerulli and the United Nations War Crimes Commission." *Northeast African Studies* 18, no. 1/2 (2018): 165–200.

De Sacy, Silvestre A. I. "Notice du livre d'Enoch." *Le Magasin encyclopédique, ou journal des sciences, des lettres et des arts* 6, no. 1 (1800): 369–98.

Dehérain, Henri. *Silvestre de Sacy et ses correspondants*. Paris: Paul Brodard, 1919.

Deplano, Valeria. *L'Africa in casa: propaganda e cultura coloniale nell'Italia fascista*. Milan: Le Monnier, 2015.
Derat, Marie-Laure. *Le domaine des rois éthiopiens (1270–1527): Espace, pouvoir et monachisme*. Paris: Éditions de la Sorbonne, 2003.
Deresse Ayenachew. "Le Kätäma: la cour et le camp royal en Éthiopie (XIVe-XVIe): espace et pouvoir." Thèse de doctorat. Université Paris 1, 2009.
———. "Territorial Expansion and Administrative Evolution under the 'Solomonic' Dynasty." In *A Companion to Medieval Ethiopia and Eritrea*, edited by Samantha Kelly, 57–85. Leiden: Brill, 2020.
Diderot, Denis, and Jean le Rond d'Alembert, eds. *Encyclopédie, ou dictionnaire raisonné des sciences, des arts et des métiers*. Paris: Briasson, 1751.
Dillmann, August. *Lexicon linguae aethiopicae cum indice latino*. Leipzig: Weigel, 1865.
Dillmann, August, and Carl Bezold. *Ethiopic Grammar, English*. Translated by James A. Crichton. 2nd ed. London: Williams and Norgate, 1907.
Dorato, Mario. "[Discours d'accueil à l'Istituto Italiano per l'Africa]." *Présence africaine* 24/25 (1959): 25.
Duca, Antonius. *Septem principum angelorum orationes cum missae eorum antiquis imaginibus*. Venice: 1543.
Earle, Thomas Foster, and Kate Lowe, eds. *Black Africans in Renaissance Europe*. Cambridge: Cambridge University Press, 2005.
El-Ariss, Tarek. "On Cooks and Crooks: Aḥmad Fāris al-Shidyāq and the Orientalists in England and France (1840s–1850s)." In *The Muslim Reception of European Orientalism*, edited by Susannah Heschel and Umar Ryad, 14–38. New York: Routledge, 2018.
Equiano, Olaudah. *The Interesting Narrative of the Life of Olaudah Equiano, or Gustavus Vassa, the African*. London: T. Wilkins, 1789.
Erasmus, Desiderius. *Ecclesiastae sive de ratione concionandi libri quatuor*. Edited by Friedrich August Klein. Leipzig: Libraria Weidmannia, 1820.
Erho, Ted M., and Loren T. Stuckenbruck. "A Manuscript History of Ethiopic Enoch." *Journal for the Study of the Pseudepigrapha* 23, no. 2 (2013): 87–133.
Esche-Ramshorn, Christiane. "Multi-Ethnic Pilgrim Centre: Sharing Sacred Space in Renaissance Rome, the Diversity of Religions and the Arts." In *Fremde in der Stadt: Ordnungen, Repräsentationen und soziale Praktiken*, edited by Peter Bell, 171–94. Frankfurt: Lang, 2010.

Euringer, Sebastian. "Das Epitaphium des Tasfa Sejon." *Oriens Christianus (3rd Series)* I (1926): 49–66.

Falchetta, Piero. *Fra Mauro's Map of the World: With a Commentary and Translations of the Inscriptions*. Turnhout: Brepols, 2006.

Febvre, Lucien. *The Problem of Unbelief in the Sixteenth Century and the Religion of Rabelais*. Translated by Beatrice Gottlieb. Cambridge, MA: Harvard University Press, 1982.

Fellman, Jack. "The First Grammar of an African Tongue." *African Studies* 44, no. 2 (1985): 197–98.

Fikru Negash Gebrekidan. "Ethiopia in Black Studies from W.E.B. Du Bois to Henry Louis Gates, Jr." *Northeast African Studies* 15, no. 1 (2015): 1–34.

Fosi, Irene. "A Proposito di nationes a Roma in età moderna: provenienza, appartenenza culturale, integrazione sociale." *Quellen und Forschungen aus Italienischen Archiven und Bibliotheken* 97, no. 1 (2017): 383–93.

Foster, Elizabeth Ann. *African Catholic: Decolonization and the Transformation of the Church*. Cambridge, MA: Harvard University Press, 2019.

Fumagalli, Giuseppe. *Bibliografia etiopica*. Milan: Hoepli, 1895.

Furey, Constance M. *Erasmus, Contarini, and the Religious Republic of Letters*. New York: Cambridge University Press, 2006.

Gamrath, Helge. *Farnese: Pomp, Power and Politics in Renaissance Italy*. Rome: "L'Erma" di Bretschneider, 2007.

Getatchew Haile. "A History of the Tabot of Atronəsä Maryam in Amhara (Ethiopia)." *Paideuma* 34 (1988): 13–22.

"A Page from the History of Däbrä Libanos of Šäwa." In *Ethiopian Studies in Honour of Amha Asfaw*, 321–410. New York: 2017.

"The Letter of Archbishops Mika'el and Gäbrə'el Concerning the Observance of Saturday." *Journal of Semitic Studies* 26, no. 1 (1981): 73–78.

Ghobrial, John-Paul. "Migration from Within and Without: In the Footsteps of Eastern Christians in the Early Modern World." *Transactions of the Royal Historical Society* 27 (2017): 153–73.

"The Archive of Orientalism and Its Keepers: Re-Imagining the Histories of Arabic Manuscripts in Early Modern Europe." *Past and Present* 230, no. 11 (2016): 90–111.

Gibbon, Edward. *The History of the Decline and Fall of the Roman Empire*. Dublin: William Hallhead, 1776.

Gill, Joseph. *The Council of Florence*. Cambridge: Cambridge University Press, 1959.

Giovio, Paolo. *Dialogo sugli uomini e le donne illustri del nostro tempo [1528]*. Edited by Franco Minonzio. Turin: Nino Aragno, 2011.

Elogia virorum bellica virtute illustrium, veris imaginibus supposita. Florence: Laurentio Torrentini, 1551.

La prima parte delle Historie del suo tempo di Mons. Paolo Giovio di Nocera. Venice: Domenico de Farri, 1555.

Pauli Iovii novocomensis episcopi nucerini historiarum sui temporis. Florence: Laurentius Torrentinus, 1550.

Girard, Aurélien. "Was an Eastern Scholar Necessarily a Cultural Broker in Early Modern Europe? Faustus Naironus (1628–1711), the Christian East, and Oriental Studies." In *Confessionalisation and Erudition in Early Modern Europe: An Episode in the History of the Humanities*, edited by Nicholas Hardy and Dmitri Levitin, 240–63. New York: Oxford University Press, 2019.

Girard, Aurélien, and Giovanni Pizzorusso. "The Maronite College in Early Modern Rome: Between the Ottoman Empire and the Republic of Letters." In *College Communities Abroad: Education, Migration, and Catholicism in Early Modern Europe*, edited by Thomas O'Connor and Liam Chambers, 174–97. Manchester: Manchester University Press, 2017.

Gleason, Elisabeth G. *Gasparo Contarini: Venice, Rome, and Reform*. Berkeley: University of California Press, 1993.

Góis, Damião de. *Fides, religio, moresque aethiopum sub imperio Preciosi Ioannis*. Louvain: Ex Officina Rutgeri Rescij, 1540.

Gomez, Michael A. *Reversing Sail: A History of the African Diaspora*. New York: Cambridge University Press, 2004.

Grafton, Anthony. *New Worlds, Ancient Texts: The Power of Tradition and the Shock of Discovery*. Cambridge: Belknap Press, 1992.

Grébaut, Sylvain. "Contribution a l'histoire du couvent éthiopien San-Stefano-dei-Mori." *Revue de l'Orient Chrétien* 26 (1927): 211–18.

"Ordre du baptême et de la confirmation dans l'église éthiopienne." *Revue de l'Orient Chrétien*, III, VI (1928/1927): 105–85.

Grébaut, Sylvain, and Eugène Tisserant. *Codices aethiopici vaticani et borgiani: Barberinianus orientalis 2, Rossianus 865*. Vatican City: Biblioteca Apostolica Vaticana, 1935.

Guha, Ranajit. *History at the Limit of World-History*. New York: Columbia University Press, 2002.

Guidi, Ignazio. "La prima stampa del Nuovo Testamento in etiopico fatta in Roma nel 1548–1549." *Archivio della Regia Società Romana di storia patria* IX (1886): 273–78.

Haberland, Eike. "Hiob Ludolf, Father of Ethiopian Studies in Europe." In *Proceedings of the Third International Conference on Ethiopian Studies*. Vol. 1, 131–36. Addis Ababa: Institute of Ethiopian Studies, 1969.

Hamilton, Alastair. "An Egyptian Traveller in the Republic of Letters: Josephus Barbatus or Abudacnus the Copt." *Journal of the Warburg and Courtauld Institutes* 57 (1994): 123–50.

The Copts and the West, 1439–1822: The European Discovery of the Egyptian Church. Oxford: Oxford University Press, 2006.

Hassen, Mohammed. "Revisiting Abba Bahrey's 'The News of the Galla.'" *The International Journal of African Historical Studies* 45, no. 2 (2012): 273–94.

The Oromo of Ethiopia: A History, 1570–1860. Cambridge: Cambridge University Press, 1990.

Hirsch, Elisabeth Feist. *Damião de Gois: the Life and Thought of a Portuguese Humanist, 1502–1574*. The Hague: Martinus Nijhoff, 1967.

Ignatius of Loyola. *Monumenta Ignatiana, ex autographis vel ex antiquioribus exemplis collecta*. Madrid: Typis G. Lopez del Horno, 1903.

Ignatius Ortiz de Urbina. "L'Etiopia e la Santa Sede nel secolo XVI." *Civiltà cattolica* IV (1934): 382–98.

Iyob, Ruth. "Reflections on African Diasporas in the Mediterranean World." In *Dimensions of African and Other Diasporas*, edited by Ruth Iyob and Franklin W. Knight, 31–51. Kingston: University of the West Indies Press, 2014.

Jorga, Nicola. "Cenni sulle relazioni tra l'Abissinia e l'Europa cattolica nei secoli XIV–XV, con un itinerario inedito del secolo XV." In *Centenario della nascita di Michele Amari*, edited by Giambattista Siragusa, 139–50. Palermo: Stabilimento tipografico Virzì, 1910.

Keller, Marcus, and Javier Irigoyen-García. "Introduction: The Dialectics of Early Modern Orientalism." In *The Dialectics of Orientalism in Early Modern Europe*, edited by Marcus Keller and Javier Irigoyen-García, 1–16. London: Palgrave, 2018.

Kelly, Samantha. "Ethiopia and Ethiopian Languages in Renaissance Italy." In *Languages and Cross-Cultural Exchange in Renaissance Italy*, edited by Alessandra Petrocchi and Joshua Brown, 331–58. Turnhout: Brepols, 2023.

"Medieval Ethiopian Diasporas." In *A Companion to Medieval Ethiopia and Eritrea*, edited by Samantha Kelly, 425–53. Leiden: Brill, 2020.

"The Curious Case of Ethiopic Chaldean: Fraud, Philology, and Cultural (Mis)Understanding in European Conceptions of Ethiopia." *Renaissance Quarterly* 68, no. 4 (2015): 1227–64.

Translating Faith: Ethiopian Pilgrims in Renaissance Rome. Cambridge, MA: Harvard University Press, 2024.

Kelly, Samantha, and Denis Nosnitsin. "The Two Yoḥannəses of Santo Stefano degli Abissini, Rome: Reconstructing Biography and Cross-Cultural Encounter through Manuscript Evidence." *Manuscript Studies* 2, no. 2 (2017): 392–426.

Kennerley, Sam. *Rome and the Maronites in the Renaissance and Reformation.* Milton: Taylor and Francis, 2021.

The Reception of John Chrysostom in Early Modern Europe: Translating and Reading a Greek Church Father from 1417 to 1624. Berlin: De Gruyter, 2023.

Keymolen, Jacob, ed. *Legatio David aethiopiae regis, ad sanctissimum D.N Clementem Papa VII.* Bologna: Iacobum Kemolen Alostensem, 1533.

ed. *L'Ambasciaria di David, re dell'Etiopia, al santissimo S. N. Clemente Papa VII.* Bologna: Giacobo Keymolen Alostese, 1533.

Kindeneh Endeg Mihretie. "Founded by, Dedicated to, and Fighting about the Holy Savior: Schism in Waldəba, a Microcosm of Factionalism in the Ethiopian Church." *Northeast African Studies* 14, no. 1 (2014): 43–66.

Kliemann, Julian. *Gesta dipinte: la grande decorazione nelle dimore italiane dal quattrocento al seicento.* Milano: Silvana Editoriale, 1993.

Kontje, Todd. *German Orientalisms.* Ann Arbor: University of Michigan Press, 2004.

Krebs, Verena. *Medieval Ethiopian Kingship, Craft, and Diplomacy with Latin Europe.* Cham: Palgrave Macmillan, 2021.

Kuntz, Marion Leathers. *Guillaume Postel, Prophet of the Restitution of All Things: His Life and Thought.* The Hague: Nijhoff, 1981.

Kur, Stanislas, ed. *Actes de Marha Krestos. 1, [Textus].* Louvain: Secrétariat du CorpusSCO, 1972.

Lee, Ralph. "The Reception and Function of 1 Enoch in the Ethiopian Orthodox Tradition." In *Rediscovering Enoch? The Antediluvian Past from the Fifteenth to Nineteenth Centuries*, edited Ariel Hessayon, Annette Yoshiko Reed, and Gabriele Boccaccini, 311–25. Leiden: Brill, 2023.

Lefevre, Renato. "Documenti e notizie su Tasfa Seyon e la sua attività romana nel sec. XVI." *Rassegna di studi etiopici* 24 (1969): 74–133.

"Giovanni Potken e la sua edizione romana del Salterio in etiopico (1513)." *La Bibliofilia* 68, no. 3 (1966): 289–308.

"La leggenda del Prete Gianni e l'Etiopia." *L'Africa italiana* 13, no. 4 (1935): 201–55.

"Ricerche sull'imolese G. B. De Brocchi: viaggiatore in Etiopia e curiale pontificio (sec. XV-XVI)." *Archivio della società romana di storia patria* 3, 12, no. 1–4 (1958): 55–118.

"Riflessi etiopici nella cultura europea del medioevo e del rinascimento." *Annali lateranensi* VIII (1944): 9–89; IX (1945): 331–444; and XI (1947): 254–342.

Terra nostra d'Africa, 1932–1935. Milano: ISPI, 1942.

Levillain, Philippe, and Deborah Blaz. *The Papacy: An Encyclopedia*. Vol. 1. New York: Routledge, 2002.

Little, Donald P. "Communal Strife in Late Mamlūk Jerusalem." *Islamic Law and Society* 6, no. 1 (1999): 69–96.

Lockman, Zachary. *Contending Visions of the Middle East: The History and Politics of Orientalism*. Cambridge: Cambridge University Press, 2004.

"Lo storiografo dell'Etiopia." *Italia coloniale* 6, no. 8 (1929): 143–45.

Ludolf, Hiob. *Iobi Ludolfi ad suam historiam aethiopicam antehac editam commentarius*. Frankfurt am Main: Zunner, 1691.

Iobi Ludolfi historia aethiopica. Frankfurt am Main: Zunner, 1681.

Jobi Ludolfi I. C. lexicon aethiopico-latinum. Edited by Johann Michael Wansleben. London: Roycroft, 1661.

Iobi Ludolfi lexicon aethiopico-latinum. 2nd ed. Frankfurt am Main: Johannem David Zunnerum, 1699.

Jobi Ludolfi J.C. grammatica aethiopica. Edited by Johann Michael Wansleben. London: Thomam Roycroft, 1661.

Makdisi, Ussama. *Age of Coexistence: The Ecumenical Frame and the Making of the Modern Arab World*. Berkeley: University of California Press, 2019.

Manning, Patrick. *The African Diaspora: A History through Culture*. New York: Columbia University Press, 2009.

Mannoni, Laura. *Una carta italiana del bacino del Nilo e dell'Etiopia del secolo XV*. Rome: Istituto di Geografia della R. Università di Roma, 1932.

Manuel. *Epistola invictissimi regis portugalliae ad Leonem X.P.M. super foedere inito cum Presbytero Ioanne aethiopiae rege*. Lisbon: 1521.

Marchand, Suzanne L. *German Orientalism in the Age of Empire: Religion, Race, and Scholarship*. Cambridge: Cambridge University Press, 2009.

Marcocci, Giuseppe. "Gli umanisti italiani e l'impero portoghese: una interpretazione della Fides, Religio, Moresque Æthiopum Di Damião de Góis." *Rinascimento* XLV (2005): 307–66.

The Globe on Paper: Writing Histories of the World in Renaissance Europe and the Americas. New York: Oxford University Press, 2020.

Martínez d'Alòs-Moner, Andreu. "Conquistadores, Mercenaries, and Missionaries: The Failed Portuguese Dominion of the Red Sea." *Northeast African Studies* 12, no. 1 (2012): 1–28.

Envoys of a Human God: The Jesuit Mission to Christian Ethiopia, 1557–1632. Leiden: Brill, 2015.

Matthiae, Guglielmo. *S. Maria degli Angeli*. Rome: Marietti, 1965.

Mauro da Leonessa. *Santo Stefano Maggiore degli Abissini e le relazioni romano-etiopiche*. Vatican City: Tipografia Poliglotta Vaticana, 1929.

Mebratu Kiros Gebru. *Miaphysite Christology: An Ethiopian Perspective*. Piscataway: Gorgias Press, 2010.

Merkle, Sebastian, ed. *Concilium Tridentinum: Diariorum, Actorum, Epistularum, Tractatum*. Freiberg: Herder, 1911.

Mickael Bethe-Sélassié. *La jeune Éthiopie: un haut fonctionnaire éthiopien, Bernahä-Marqos Wäldä-Tsadeq, 1892–1943*. Paris: L'Harmattan, 2009.

Mufti, Aamir. *Forget English! Orientalisms and World Literature*. Cambridge, MA: Harvard University Press, 2016.

Natta, Gabriele. "L'enigma dell'Etiopia nel rinascimento italiano: Ludovico Beccadelli tra inquietudini religiose e orizzonti globali." *Rinascimento* 55 (2015): 275–309.

Newitt, Malyn. *A History of Portuguese Overseas Expansion, 1400–1668*. London: Routledge, 2005.

Northrup, David. *Africa's Discovery of Europe: 1450–1850*. New York: Oxford University Press, 2002.

Nosnitsin, Denis. "'A History That Was Found' a Recent Chapter in the Historiography of Däbrä Libanos." *Africana Bulletin* 54 (2006): 35–53.

O'Malley, John W. *The First Jesuits*. Cambridge, MA: Harvard University Press, 1993.

Otele, Olivette. *African Europeans: An Untold History*. London: Basic Books, 2022.

Paschini, Pio. "Un cardinale editore: Marcello Cervini." In *Miscellanea di scritti di bibliografia ed erudizione in memoria di Luigi Ferrari*, edited by Luigi Ferrari, 383–413. Florence: Olschki, 1952.

Pastor, Ludwig. *The History of the Popes*. Edited by Ralph Francis Kerr. Vol. 13. London: Kegan Paul, Trench, Trubner, 1924.

Pennec, Hervé. *Des jésuites au royaume du Prêtre Jean (Ethiopie). Stratégies, rencontres et tentatives d'implantation, 1495–1633*. Paris: Centre Culturel Calouste Gulbenkian, 2003.

Perruchon, Jules François Célestin, ed. *Les chroniques de Zar'a Yâ`eqôb et de Ba'eda Mâryâm, Rois d'Éthiope de 1434 à 1478*. Paris: É. Bouillon, 1893.

Pescatello, Ann M. "The African Presence in Portuguese India." *Journal of Asian History* 11, no. 1 (1977): 26–48.

Petrowicz, Gregorio. *Il Patriarca di Ecimiazin Stefano V Salmastetzi: 1541–1552*. Rome: Pont. institutum orientalium studiorum, 1962.

Petry, Yvonne. *Gender, Kabbalah, and the Reformation: The Mystical Theology of Guillaume Postel (1510–1581)*. Leiden: Brill, 2004.

Pigli, Mario [Gihâd]. *La civiltà italiana e l'Etiopia*. Rome: Dante Alighieri, 1935.

Postel, Guillaume. *Des histoires orientales* [...]. Paris: Hierosme de Marnef, 1575.

———. *Guillaume Postel (1510–1581) et son interprétation du candélabre de Moyse: en hébreu, latin, italien et français, avec une introduction et des notes*. Edited by François Secret. Nieuwkoop: B. de Graaf, 1966.

———. *Linguarum duodecim characteribus differentium alphabetum, introductio, ac legendi modus longè facilimus* [...]. Paris: Dionysium Lescuier, 1538.

Potken, Johannes. *Psalterium in quatuor linguis: Hebraea, greca, chaldaea, latina*. Cologne: Soter, 1518.

Potken, Johannes, and Tomas Wäldä Samu'él. *Psalterium David et cantica aliqua in lingua chaldea*. Rome: Marcellus Silber, 1513.

Pouillon, François, Alain Messaoudi, Dietrich Rauchenberger, and Oumelbanine Zhiri, eds. *Léon l'Africain*. Paris: Éditions Karthala, 2020.

Proverbio, Delio Vania. "Santo Stefano degli Abissini. Una breve rivisitazione." *La parola del passato* 66 (2011): 50–68.

Pugliatti, Teresa. *Giulio Mazzoni e la decorazione a Roma nella cerchia di Daniele da Volterra*. Rome: Istituto poligrafico e Zecca dello Stato, Libreria dello Stato, 1984.

Puglisi, Giuseppe. *Chi è? dell'Eritrea, 1952. Dizionario biografico, con una cronologia*. Asmara: Agenzia Regina, 1952.

Quaranta, Chiara. *Marcello II Cervini (1501–1555): riforma della chiesa, concilio, inquisizione*. Bologna: Il Mulino, 2010.

Raineri, Osvaldo. *Inventario dei manoscritti Cerulli etiopici*. Vatican City: Biblioteca Apostolica Vaticana, 2004.

———. "Gli studi etiopici nell'età di Giovio." In *Atti del convegno Paolo Giovio: il rinascimento e la memoria: Como, 3–5 giugno 1983*, edited by T. C. Price Zimmerman, 117–31. Como: Presso la Società a Villa Gallia, 1985.

Raineri, Osvaldo, and Ilaria Delsere. *Chiesa di S. Stefano dei Mori: vicende edilizie e personaggi*. Vatican City: Edizioni Capitolo Vaticano, 2015.

Ramusio, Giovanni Battista. *Delle navigationi et viaggi*. Vol. 1. Venetia: Giunti, 1550.

Relaño, Francesc. *The Shaping of Africa: Cosmographic Discourse and Cartographic Science in Late Medieval and Early Modern Europe*. Burlington: Ashgate, 2002.

Sachet, Paolo. *Publishing for the Popes: The Roman Curia and the Use of Printing (1527–1555)*. Leiden: Brill, 2020.

Said, Edward. *Orientalism*. New York: Pantheon Books, 1978.

Sala Stampa della Santa Sede. "Udienza alla comunità del Pontificio Collegio Etiopico in Vaticano." *Bollettino*, January 11, 2020. https://press.vatican.va/content/salastampa/it/bollettino/pubblico/2020/01/11/0020/00041.html.

Salmeron, Alfonso. *Epistolae Alphonsi Salmeronis Societatis Jesu. Tomus primus*. Madrid: Typis Gabrielis Lopez del Horno, 1906.

Salvadore, Matteo. "African Cosmopolitanism in the Early Modern Mediterranean: The Diasporic Life of Yohannes, the Ethiopian Pilgrim Who Became a Counter-Reformation Bishop." *The Journal of African History* 58, no. 1 (2017): 61–83.

"Between the Red Sea Slave Trade and the Goa Inquisition: The Odyssey of Gabriel, a Sixteenth-Century Ethiopian Jew." *Journal of World History* 31, no. 2 (2020): 327–60.

"Europe's Other Ethiopian Diaspora: The Ordeals of António, an Enslaved Muslim in Early Modern Lisbon." *International Journal of African Historical Studies* 57, no. 1 (2024): 35–59.

"Gaining the Heart of Prester John: Loyola's Blueprint for Ethiopia in Three Key Documents." *World History Connected* 10, no. 3 (2013). http://worldhistoryconnected.press.illinois.edu/10.3/forum_salvadore.html.

The African Prester John and the Birth of Ethiopian–European Relations 1402–1555. New York: Routledge, 2017.

"The Ethiopian Age of Exploration: Prester John's Discovery of Europe, 1306–1458." *The Journal of World History* 21, no. 4 (2010): 593–627.

Salvadore, Matteo, and James De Lorenzi. "An Ethiopian Scholar in Tridentine Rome: Täsfa Ṣeyon and the Birth of Orientalism." *Itinerario* 45, no. 1 (2021): 17–46.

Samuel Asghedom. "Contributo dell'ospizio di Santo Stefano degli Abissini agli studi etiopici in Europa." In *IV Congresso internazionale di studi etiopici (Roma, 10–15 aprile 1972)*, Vol. 1, 389–404. Rome: Accademia Nazionale dei Lincei, 1974.

Santus, Cesare. "L'accoglienza e il controllo dei pellegrini orientali a Roma." *Mélanges de l'École française de Rome-Moyen Âge* 131–132 (2019): 447–59.

"Tra la chiesa di Sant'Atanasio e il Sant'Uffizio: note sulla presenza greca a Roma in età moderna." In *Chiese e nationes a Roma: dalla Scandianavia ai Balcani, Secoli XV-XVIII*, edited by Antal Molnár, Giovanni Pizzorusso, and Matteo Sanfilippo, 193–224. Rome: Viella, 2017.

"Wandering Lives: Eastern Christian Pilgrims, Alms-Collectors and 'Refugees' in Early Modern Rome." In *A Companion to Religious Minorities in Early Modern Rome*, edited by Matthew Coneys Wainright and Emily Michelson, 237–71. Leiden: Brill, 2020.

Sassetti, Angelo Sacchetti. *La vita e gli scritti di Mariano Vittori*. Rieti: Tipografia S. Trinchi, 1917.

Secret, François. "Guillaume Postel et les études arabes à la renaissance." *Arabica* 9, no. 1 (1962): 21–36.

Sequeria, Diogo Lopes de, and Pero Gomes Teixeira. *The Discovery of Abyssinia by the Portuguese in 1520*. Edited by Henry Thomas. Translated by Armando Cortesão. London: British Museum, 1938.

Sharkey, Heather. *A History of Muslims, Christians, and Jews in the Middle East*. Cambridge: Cambridge University Press, 2017.

Shelemay, Kay Kaufman, and Peter Jeffery, eds. *Ethiopian Christian Liturgical Chant, Part 3*. Madison: A-R Editions, 1997.

Silva, Luiz Augusto Rebello da. *Corpo diplomatico Portuguez*. Lisbon: Academia Real das Sciencias, 1865.

Simmel, Georg. "The Stranger." In *The Sociology of Georg Simmel*. Translated by Kurt Wolff, 402–8. New York: Free Press, 1950.

Solomon Gebreyes, ed. *Chronicle of King Gälawdewos (1540–1559)*. Louvain: Peeters, 2019.

Somigli, Teodosio. *Etiopia francescana nei documenti dei secoli XVII e XVIII*. Vol. 1. Florence: Quaracchi, 1928.

Subrahmanyam, Sanjay. "Connected Histories: Notes towards a Reconfiguration of Early Modern Eurasia." *Modern Asian Studies* 31 (1997): 735–62.

"On World Historians in the Sixteenth Century." *Representations* 91, no. 1 (2005): 26–57.

The Career and Legend of Vasco Da Gama. Cambridge: Cambridge University Press, 1998.

The Portuguese Empire in Asia, 1500–1700: A Political and Economic History. Oxford: Wiley-Blackwell, 2012.

Taddesse Tamrat. *Church and State in Ethiopia, 1270–1527*. Oxford: Clarendon Press, 1972.

"Evangelizing the Evangelized: The Root Problem between Missions and the Ethiopian Orthodox Church." In *The Missionary Factor in Ethiopia [. . .]*, edited by Getatchew Haile, Aasulv Lande, and Samuel Rubenson, 17–30. Frankfurt: Peter Lang, 1998.

[Täsfa Ṣeyon] Petrus Abbas. *Modus baptizandi, preces et benedictiones, quibus Ecclesia Ethiopum utitur [. . .]*. Rome: Antonium Bladum, 1549.

[Täsfa Ṣeyon] Petrus Ethyops. *Testamentum Novum cum Epistola Pauli ad Hebreos tantum cum concordantiis Evangelistarum Eusebii & numeratione omnium verborum eorundem* [...]. Rome: Valerius Doricus, 1548.
Taylor, Christopher. "Tracing the Paths of an Imaginary King." *Studi e materiali di storia delle religioni* 89 (2023): 122–41.
Tedeschi, Salvatore. "L'Etiopia di Poggio Bracciolini." *Africa* 48, no. 3 (1993): 333–58.
——. "Profilo storico di Dayr as-Sultan." *Journal of Ethiopian Studies* 2, no. 2 (1964): 92–160.
Täklä Maryam Sämḥaray Sälim. *La messe éthiopienne*. Rome: École Typographique "Pie X," 1937.
Teshale Tibebu. "Ethiopia: The 'Anomaly' and 'Paradox' of Africa." *Journal of Black Studies* 2, no. 4 (1996): 414–430.
Tinguely, Frédéric. *L'écriture du Levant à la Renaissance: enquête sur les voyageurs français dans l'empire de Soliman le magnifique*. Geneva: Droz, 1995.
Valenziano, Crispino. "Introduzione alla historia dell'erettione della Chiesa di S. Maria degli Angioli [...]." *Ho Theologos* 3 (1976): 29–172.
Vedovato, Giuseppe. *Gli accordi italo-etiopici dell'agosto 1928*. Florence: Poligrafico Toscano, 1956.
Victorius, Marianus. *Chaldeae, seu aethiopicae linguae institutiones*. Rome: V. Doricus, 1552.
Wheeler, Brannon. "Guillaume Postel and the Primordial Origins of the Middle East." *Method and Theory in the Study of Religion* 25 (2013): 244–63.
Whiteway, Richard Stephen, ed. *The Portuguese Expedition to Abyssinia in 1541–1543 as Narrated by Castanhoso*. London: The Hakluyt Society, 1902.
Wilkinson, Robert J. *Orientalism, Aramaic, and Kabbalah in the Catholic Reformation: The First Printing of the Syriac New Testament*. Leiden: Brill, 2007.
Wolk-Simon, Linda. "'The Finger of God Is Here': The Farnese, the Jesuits, and the Gesù." In *The Holy Name: Art of the Gesù*, edited by Linda Wolk-Simon. Philadelphia: Saint Joseph's University Press, 2018.
Wright, Elizabeth R. *The Epic of Juan Latino: Dilemmas of Race and Religion in Renaissance Spain*. Toronto: University of Toronto Press, 2016.
Ze'evi, Dror. *An Ottoman Century: The District of Jerusalem in the 1600s*. Albany: State University of New York Press, 1996.
Zemon Davis, Natalie. *Trickster Travels: A Sixteenth-Century Muslim between Worlds*. New York: Hill and Wang, 2006.
Zuurmond, Rochus. *Novum Testamentum Aethiopice: The Synoptic Gospels*. Vol. 1. Wiesbaden: Franz Steiner, 1989.

Cambridge Elements

The Renaissance

John Henderson
Birkbeck, University of London, and Wolfson College, University of Cambridge

John Henderson is Emeritus Professor of Italian Renaissance History at Birkbeck, University of London, and Emeritus Fellow of Wolfson College, University of Cambridge. His recent publications include *Florence Under Siege: Surviving Plague in an Early Modern City* (2019), *Plague and the City*, edited with Lukas Engelmann and Christos Lynteris (2019), and *Representing Infirmity: Diseased Bodies in Renaissance Italy*, edited with Fredrika Jacobs and Jonathan K. Nelson (2021). He is also the author of *Piety and Charity in Late Medieval Florence* (1994); *The Great Pox: The French Disease in Renaissance Europe*, with Jon Arrizabalaga and Roger French (1997); and *The Renaissance Hospital: Healing the Body and Healing the Soul* (2006). Forthcoming publications include a Cambridge Element, *Representing and Experiencing the Great Pox in Renaissance Italy* (2023).

Jonathan K. Nelson
Syracuse University Florence

Jonathan K. Nelson teaches Italian Renaissance Art at Syracuse University Florence and is research associate at the Harvard Kennedy School. His books include *Filippino Lippi* (2004, with Patrizia Zambrano); *Leonardo e la reinvenzione della figura femminile* (2007), *The Patron's Payoff: Conspicuous Commissions in Italian Renaissance Art* (2008, with Richard J. Zeckhauser), *Filippino Lippi* (2022); and he co-edited *Representing Infirmity. Diseased Bodies in Renaissance Italy* (2021). He co-curated museum exhibitions dedicated to Michelangelo (2002), Botticelli and Filippino (2004), Robert Mapplethorpe (2009), and Marcello Guasti (2019), and two online exhibitions about Bernard Berenson (2012, 2015). Forthcoming publications include a Cambridge Element, *Risks in Renaissance Art: Production, Purchase, Reception* (2023).

Assistant Editor
Sarah McBryde, *Birkbeck, University of London*

Editorial Board
Wendy Heller, *Scheide Professor of Music History, Princeton University*
Giorgio Riello, *Chair of Early Modern Global History, European University Institute, Florence*
Ulinka Rublack, *Professor of Early Modern History, St Johns College, University of Cambridge*
Jane Tylus, *Andrew Downey Orrick Professor of Italian and Professor of Comparative Literature, Yale University*

About the Series
Timely, concise, and authoritative, Elements in the Renaissance showcases cutting-edge scholarship by both new and established academics. Designed to introduce students, researchers, and general readers to key questions in current research, the volumes take multi-disciplinary and transnational approaches to explore the conceptual, material, and cultural frameworks that structured Renaissance experience.

Cambridge Elements

The Renaissance

Elements in the Series

Paradoxes of Inequality in Renaissance Italy
Samuel K. Cohn, Jr.

The World in Dress: Costume Books across Italy, Europe, and the East
Giulia Calvi

Cinderella's Glass Slipper: Towards a Cultural History of Renaissance Materialities
Genevieve Warwick

The Renaissance on the Road: Mobility, Migration and Cultural Exchange
Rosa Salzberg

Measuring in the Renaissance: An Introduction
Emanuele Lugli

Elite Women and the Italian Wars, 1494–1559
Susan Broomhall and Carolyn James

Risks in Renaissance Art: Production, Purchase, and Reception
Jonathan K. Nelson and Richard J. Zeckhauser

Senses of Space in the Early Modern World
Nicholas Terpstra

Plague, Towns and Monarchy in Early Modern France
Neil Murphy

The French Disease in Renaissance Italy: Representation and Experience
John Henderson

Who Owns Literature?: Early Modernity's Orphaned Texts
Jane Tylus

The Many Lives of Täsfa Ṣeyon: An Ethiopian Intellectual in Early Modern Rome
Matteo Salvadore, James De Lorenzi and Deresse Ayenachew Woldetsadik

A full series listing is available at: www.cambridge.org/EREN